TOO BIG TO LOSE

Oct 19, 2023

To Jason, thank you for all you do for the State of Hawaii.

Raymond

TOO BIG TO LOSE

A SMALL FARMER'S TEN YEAR BATTLE AGAINST DUPONT

RAYMOND KAWAMATA

Too Big to Lose

FIRST EDITION

ISBN: 978-1-7365253-0-2
978-1-7365253-1-9 (eBook)

Library of Congress Control Number: 2021901182

MP
Margaux Press

This memoir is a work of creative nonfiction.
The events are portrayed to the very best of the
author's memory. Neither the author nor publisher
make any representations or warranties as to accuracy.

To those who wanted me to win,
and to those who wanted me to lose.

FOREWORD

I first met Raymond Kawamata in the fall of 1992 at his father's home in Kawaihae, a coastal fishing village about ten miles from their rose farm in Waimea on the Big Island of Hawaii. I was a young attorney, recently hired by the law firm that would represent the Kawamatas in their long, protracted fight for justice against one of the largest chemical companies in the world. A few months earlier, the Kawamatas had filed a lawsuit against DuPont for damages to their farm caused by an agricultural product called Benlate. DuPont was facing similar damage claims by numerous Hawaii farmers and by thousands of other growers throughout the United States and abroad. I was still pretty green and I had no idea what I was getting into. I certainly had no idea of the lengths to which DuPont would go to defend itself.

Right away, however, I got a pretty good idea of what kind of man Raymond was. He was smart, that much was clear. He and his eighty-year-old father grilled me on my qualifications and background, but the grilling was gentle. And not without humor. I left our initial meeting with a smile on my face and a good feeling about Raymond, his father, and their down-to-earth aloha spirit.

If you know Raymond, "not without humor," is a good way to describe him, if a little understated. The truth is, through the long and tortured course of the case, Raymond would have me laughing a hell of a lot, and often just when I needed it most. His case was one that begged for comic relief. Millions of dollars were at stake. So was Raymond's very livelihood. All of us working on behalf of Kawamata Farms—the partners of the law firm, the additional attorney we brought in, the entire staff—we all felt the weight of the responsibility we carried. We all had sleepless nights.

The thing about the case that sticks with me the most is the enormous commitment of time it required by everyone involved. It was all-consuming. You'll read in here about the sacrifices made. The case took years to play out. During the early days of the case, DuPont settled with numerous farmers. But back then, back when Raymond would have entertained the idea of resolving his claim as well, DuPont refused to settle with Kawamata Farms. DuPont needed an example case, someone to squash. They chose Raymond and went to war. Raymond chose to fight back.

As the new kid, I ended up doing a lot of the legal research and legwork. I learned more working on Raymond's case than I learned in three years of law school and five previous years of legal experience combined. I worked hard. I wanted to do right by our client. I needed to do right by the partners, too, who had put their faith in me the day they hired me with Raymond's case in mind. Lead counsel

Stan Roehrig, in particular, could be a tough taskmaster. Sometimes he could be a downright son of a bitch. Looking back, however, a downright son of a bitch was just what this case required. DuPont, as you'll read in this book, would try everything under the sun, ethical or not, to make the case go their direction. They had no shortage of resources. Money was no object and the goal was to essentially starve out the Kawamatas along with their attorneys. This was not a case for the faint of heart.

While Stan stayed on top of me to make sure I wasn't screwing up, Raymond stayed on top of Stan. He asked a lot of smart questions about why we were doing certain things. He was involved more than most clients, but then again, some of that had to do with the nature of the case. You'll read about the legal discovery process and about the hundreds of thousands of documents that DuPont dumped on our law office that we were forced to comb through to find the proverbial needle in a haystack—evidence that Benlate was dangerously defective, that it had caused billions of dollars in damages to farms in Hawaii and elsewhere, and that DuPont had known all this for years. As it happened, we would ultimately uncover many needles that DuPont had gone to the ends of the earth to keep buried.

The case required a lot of counsel–client interaction, and we met constantly with Raymond and Stan Tomono, another Big Island grower we also represented. There were countless court motions filed and hearings held in front of the judge who presided over the case, and I remember many evenings standing in the parking lot of the courthouse with us attorneys explaining to Raymond the legal subtleties of what had just happened inside the courtroom. In the end, Raymond almost always deferred to our expertise. But you'll read about the time he dug his heels in and told us in no uncertain terms that he was refusing to settle, risking an outcome that could have jeopardized all of our livelihoods. We respected the decision, however, as much as we respected the man who made it. And I knew that win or lose, Raymond was going to be a friend of mine when the whole sordid mess was over.

During the case, I learned a lot from Stan Roehrig, and I learned a lot from his law partner Andy Wilson, the good cop, as Raymond will tell you, to Stan's bad cop. I owe a huge debt of gratitude to both Stan and Andy for having faith in me as a person and as a young lawyer. And for teaching me how to practice law—the right way. I owe a debt of gratitude to Steve Cox as well, the outside attorney we brought in to help on our side. But I learned a lot from Raymond, too. About dignity. About integrity. About grace under pressure. Maybe the worst part of the whole thing is that such a bad set of circumstances should befall such a good guy. I'd like to think we helped even the score a little, but I think you'll find, as you read Raymond's book, that when it comes to the American judicial system, justice isn't always properly served, even when it looks like it has been.

Raymond's case brings to mind actor Tom Hanks' answer on the witness stand in the movie *Philadelphia* when asked what he liked most about being a lawyer: "Every now and again, not often, but occasionally, you get to be a part of justice being done." I've dedicated my professional career to the law, and I think our country has the best system there is but that does not make it perfect, and it certainly does not guarantee that justice is done. It's hard to argue with Raymond's assertion, born of firsthand experience, that our system is, in fact, very far from perfect. He'll tell you in his book that it's broken. I wouldn't go that far, but I can appreciate his position. Based on where Raymond has been, the man has every right to come to that conclusion and I'm not even going to try to argue with it. I recommend reading the pages that follow and making up your own mind about our country's supposed ideals of fairness and justice when you take on a corporate giant in an American court of law.

To Raymond, I'll just say thanks for being such a great client, the kind of man a guy is proud to go to war with.

Kris LaGuire, Esq.

HILO, HAWAII
JANUARY, 2021

ONE
The Life of the Land

"Mr. Kawamata, why are the roses so brown on the outside?"

It was one of the ladies who worked for me on the farm. I looked closely at the bridal pink roses she had cut that morning. She was right. Others were the same way, with the same discoloration. It wasn't as bad on the stronger red variety, mostly because it wasn't as noticeable against the deep red color, but on the lighter variety it was obvious, so obvious as to render them unmarketable. This was disconcerting, to say the least. We had over 100,000 plants and were harvesting between 8,000 and 12,000 roses per day. It was how we made our living.

At Kawamata Farms in Waimea on the Big Island of Hawaii, we had been growing roses for twenty years. The only time I'd had a similar problem was several years before when a fungicide named Pipron burned some of my plants. I'd complained to the distributor, United Agri Products in nearby Hilo, who ultimately put me in touch with Elanco, the manufacturer. Elanco took samples of the chemical and admitted they'd misformulated it and promptly replaced it. It was a stand-up thing to do, the kind of thing you'd hope any manufacturer would do. They had made a mistake and they corrected it. Then, they went above and beyond. In appreciation for my business and for the fact that I'd been a loyal customer, they agreed to sell me directly whatever additional Pipron I'd need at half the price. What I didn't know at the time was that this didn't sit well with United Agri Products who, as distributor, was now cut out of my future Pipron purchases.

Despite that experience, it didn't initially occur to me that the discoloration problem with the roses that morning was a chemical or formulation issue. I assumed it was something I did wrong. I've noticed this characteristic with farmers in general. If our crops aren't growing as they should, we think we've misapplied a pesticide or fungicide. Or maybe the climatic conditions weren't right. Maybe it was too hot or maybe it was too cloudy, conditions we somehow should have accounted for. In this case, I immediately presumed that I had misused the adjuvant I'd added to the fungicide that I had sprayed on my plants several days prior. An adjuvant is a chemical used to enhance the effectiveness of whatever you're spraying on your plants, whether it's a pesticide, herbicide or, in my case, a fungicide. It helps to better distribute the substance, helps it spread out on the leaves. Clearly, I must have screwed something up with the application. Did I use too much?

It certainly never occurred to me that the problem would have been the fungicide itself. After all, I'd used Benlate for years. It was manufactured by DuPont, a household name you could trust. They'd been around forever. Indeed, versions of Benlate could be found in the garden department of any hardware store. It was as safe to use as an ordinary can of Raid.

After that day, I began paying closer attention to how I was using the adjuvant. I was extra careful and made sure I was following the manufacturer's recommendations to the letter. As time went along, however, I continued to have the same discoloration problem with the roses, despite the fact that I ultimately removed the adjuvant altogether. It took a while, but I eventually excluded myself as the source of the problem. It wasn't the application; I'd done nothing wrong.

It didn't seem probable that the adjuvant could have been the issue given that I was no longer using it, but I was clueless as to what else it could be. Consequently, I had the adjuvant tested in a lab. Sure enough, the results came back stating that it had not been formulated to the specifications of the label. There was much too high a percentage of alcohol. With the mystery apparently solved, I reported my findings to United Agri Products, whom I was still buying from. Not that it mattered at the time, but in addition to the adjuvant, United Agri was selling me the Benlate, too.

Before long, I was visited by William Schaller, the president of Loveland Industries, manufacturer of the adjuvant and a wholly owned subsidiary of United Agri. He agreed with my lab's assessment of the formula and told me to send him an estimate for the damages, which, by then, were up to $30,000. Like Elanco, Loveland was stand-up, too. Schaller assured me the money wouldn't be a problem and to call him personally anytime there was anything he could help with. I thanked him for his prompt attention and his offer to make things right. The matter, though an inconvenience, seemed settled.

But weeks went by without Loveland making good. And then months. The damage to my roses continued unabated. Before long, the financial loss was above $80,000. I called Schaller who told me he couldn't talk to me and directed me to the law firm in Oahu that they'd hired. The company had lawyered-up. Why? The lawyer in Oahu told me the manager of United Agri Products in Hilo had recommended that Loveland not settle with me. Apparently, he'd passed along the Pipron story. "Kawamata's just looking for a payoff," he must have said. "He's made trouble before. He's a habitual complainer."

Only later would I discover what the real issue was. United Agri Products was lawyering-up, too. This was much bigger than $30,000 or even $80,000. And it was much bigger than one rose farm in Waimea, Hawaii.

In the meantime, getting nowhere fast, I needed to do something. I'm not a guy who likes to take legal action, but my crop, my livelihood, was dying around me. And now that lawyers were involved, I knew that any hopes for a quick resolution were fading fast. I called a friend of mine,

Sandra Schutte, a lawyer with the firm of Roehrig, Roehrig, Wilson, Hara, Schutte, and DeSilva in Hilo. Sandra said she was leaving the firm to start her own practice. She was too busy with the move to take my case, but referred me to fellow attorneys Andy Wilson and Stan Roehrig. I knew Stan from way back; when he was just a young guy, he used to go fishing with my father. I knew Stan could be tough. He'd built quite a reputation over the course of his career. He successfully fought against the development of a little corner of Kawaihae Harbor where we all used to get our bait fish. He also fought against development in Honoli'i where he surfed. He was a natural fighter and that had helped make him a successful plaintiffs' attorney.

Stan began negotiations with Loveland and I hoped for a quick settlement so that I could get on with the business of growing roses. But around this time, I had a strange visit. A DuPont representative from Oahu by the name of Alan Teshima came by to test my soil. I didn't know why and Teshima didn't say, but I figured it had something to do with the case against Loveland. Somehow, DuPont must have been involved. Teshima came back with a memo that stated he'd found the presence of atrazine in the soil. Atrazine is a herbicide, often used on sugar cane farms. It's a weed killer, essentially. I'd never used it in my life. Why in the world was there atrazine in my soil?

Around this time, I heard from Stan. He and Andy had been doing some digging. Apparently, there was reason to believe the problem was not with Loveland's adjuvant after all. This, then, explained the stonewalling and the lawyering-up. The problem was with the Benlate—DuPont's Benlate. And this explained the presence of Teshima. As it happens, other cases had been popping up around the country. Other farmers were having problems with their crops, too. Lots of farmers.

We filed suit against both DuPont, the manufacturer, and United Agri Products, the distributor.

This outwardly simple legal action would begin a chain of events I would never have thought possible. My initial expectation was that DuPont would settle. Maybe they'd pay me $80,000 for my damages, maybe something less. I'd pick up where I left off and go back about my business. The whole incident would be a short-lived nuisance and nothing more. How could anyone in their right minds have anticipated what would ultimately transpire? There would be months and months of pretrial motions culminating, at last, in a full-blown jury trial. There would be lengthy appeals. We would learn of other problems with Benlate, including birth defects. There would be attorneys—an army of them—in thousand-dollar suits. The $80,000 action would rise to over $30 *million*. Our case would land in the state Supreme Court. Attention to the case would go national. And the outcome? Beyond belief. Most of it would play out in a tiny, outdated courtroom in a small Hawaiian town. Through it all, I would learn more than I ever wanted to know about our legal system. About big business. About deep pockets. About what passes for "justice." What I learned wasn't pretty.

What started as a relatively straightforward matter involving $30,000 worth of damage to some roses would end up costing me ten years of my life and a marriage. Others would pay a cost, too. The amount of time and money eaten up by this one case would be astonishing. At one point, my attorneys, working on contingency, were in so deep they had to stop taking on other clients and mortgage their personal residences. Stan Roehrig and Andy Wilson had exactly one case. Mine. They went all in, betting everything on a single hand and that hand was Kawamata Farms.

Recently, someone asked me if, looking back, it was all worth it. It's a good question. I've thought a lot about that question. I have an answer and the answer comes with an explanation and that explanation is this book. Was it worth it? First, you'll need to know the whole story. That's going to mean taking a hard look at our country's system of jurisprudence. Like me, you might not like what you see. I went into the experience naïve and, boy, did I get an education. But let me not get too far ahead of myself. Let's start at the beginning, back in the days of a still-innocent farmer in a land of paradise, when life was simple. "*Ua mau ke ea o ka aina i ka pono*," reads Hawaii's state motto. "The life of the land is perpetuated in righteousness."

TWO
Kawamata Farms

Farmer wasn't my first choice, even though the option presented itself early. I always figured I'd be a lawyer or some other kind of professional. Sometimes, I think I still don't know what I want to be. Maybe one of these years, I'll figure it out.

My father, founder of Kawamata Farms, was a farmer, but only part-time. His first love was fishing, something he tried to pass along to me, but I was prone to seasickness and never felt the enthusiasm he did. Dad loved boats. He used to tell the story of how, when he was a young man, his boat was enlisted by the United States Navy. He was living on the island of Oahu, before the Second World War, before the attack on Pearl Harbor, and the Navy hired him to tow a target boat behind his own boat a few hundred yards offshore. The Navy would fire their five-inch, 51-caliber guns at the target boat, but even though the towline was long and there was a considerable distance between the vessels, a shell would sometimes land just a little too close to my father's boat for comfort. One time, he got drenched from the spray of an errant shell and immediately motored on in, telling the commander, "This is too dangerous. I'm not going back out there unless one of your officers comes with me." Someone was chosen to be the lucky person to accompany Dad, but when another wayward shell exploded in the water close to Dad's boat, the officer shrieked and screamed for Dad to immediately head for shore. That was the end of target practice for the day.

Dad's parents, my grandparents, came from Japan and settled on Oahu, working as farmers on a plantation. The apparent idea was to save enough money to return to Japan, but I imagine the war put an end to those thoughts. I'm sure there could not have been much left of their lives in Japan. Or maybe they didn't go back because they never earned enough money to do so. Or maybe it was a little of both. Whatever the reason, they stayed on Oahu. They sent Dad to school with the idea of him becoming an accountant. His brothers had a business and my father was to become a part of it, working for the family. But Dad had other ideas. For one thing, he hated accounting. He kept his boat and became a professional fisherman instead.

Eventually, Dad met Mom, they married and had eight children, all girls except for one boy—me. When I was eight, Dad moved our family to the Big Island, the Island of Hawaii. True to its nickname, it's the biggest of the island chain. In fact, it's surface area is greater than all the other Hawaiian islands combined. But it's not nearly as populous as Oahu where Honolulu is, and it was even less populous back in those days. The little town of Waimea, where we moved, was a rural town on the north side of the island, around twenty miles or so from the Mauna Kea volcano. It's a town with two names. It's also called Kamuela to distinguish it from two other Waimeas, one on Oahu and one on Kauai. The postal service insisted on the second name to lessen the confusion, but the locals didn't want to give up the original. Hence, a town with two names.

Waimea or Kamuela, it sits at 2,760 feet above sea level. The air is cool and crisp. In those days, it was populated mostly by farmers and cattle ranchers. People still rode on horseback and the town had a single road that ran past a general store. Our house had no electricity and my mother would cook on a kerosene stove in the kitchen. My father's reason for moving us there remains a little hazy to me, but I believe it was to get us away from the plantation community of Oahu at the time. He had grown up in it and was afraid of becoming an inevitable part of the social class of the laborers. It was hard to break out of. More particularly, I think he wanted his daughters to have the chance to meet other kinds of men—men with higher standing and brighter prospects than could be found among the laborers of Oahu, although in the small town of Waimea, the pickings weren't necessarily any better.

Dad fished out of a local port, taking me with him from time to time and tying a strong cord around my waist so I wouldn't be swept overboard in the frequently rough waters. The length of the cord was such that I could only venture a certain distance from the wheelhouse. I probably would have liked fishing if it hadn't been for the constant seasickness. No matter how many times I accompanied my father, I never was able to acquire my sea legs. It was near-constant nausea. Whatever it was that allowed Dad to remain as comfortable in six-foot swells as on flat land, I did not inherit.

Unfortunately, the fishing business was not especially profitable. Dad was a skilled fisherman, bringing in yellowfin, skipjack, mahi mahi, wahoo, and more, but the small population of our area meant the market was limited. Often, he sold to fish peddlers who came by the docks and who would resell the fish, but the prices were always low and it was hard to make a decent profit. It had been different in Oahu where the wholesale market around Honolulu was larger and more sophisticated. So, to make ends meet and feed his family, my father started farming. And thus began Kawamata Farms, a business established more or less by default.

The farm was a family affair and we all helped out—Dad, Mom, my sisters, and me. We grew a variety of vegetables and flowers, including carnations which were in demand by the lei makers. Because of the dry months of the Big Island, our farming was largely just a seasonal undertaking for many years, but eventually, my father installed an irrigation system which meant we could farm year-round.

Still, Dad never gave up the fishing business, which meant that as I got older, I took more and more responsibility for the farm. This was fine by me. I enjoyed farming and loved our little family farm. By the time I graduated high school, I had decided I wanted to take some college courses in agronomy. My decision to go to college wasn't anything I'd given too much thought to. Going into my senior year, college hadn't really occurred to me. Then one day a friend asked me how much I'd been studying for the SAT tests. "The what?" I asked. I hadn't even heard of them. Soon, other friends were talking about these SAT tests and so I signed up to take them, too. Having done that, the idea hit me that I could go to college and I sent out a few applications.

Initially wanting to remain in Hawaii, I applied to Church College in Oahu. Today it's known as Brigham Young University–Hawaii. Then, as now, it was a Mormon school. I didn't know this at the time. Not being a Mormon, I didn't stand much of a chance and so it should not have come as a surprise that my application was rejected. I suppose I could have gone to the University of Hawaii in Honolulu, but some friends had been accepted to California Polytechnic State University in San Luis Obispo, California. The school had a well-respected agronomy program and besides knowing people there, I liked the idea of seeing something of the mainland. As much as I liked the farm, it was exciting to think about getting out of our little Hawaiian town. California seemed like an exotic and romantic land. Funny how one thinks of one's own home. Words like exotic and romantic no doubt come to mind for people on the mainland when thinking about Hawaii.

I applied to Cal Poly and was accepted. The only thing that made the move potentially difficult was that, in the meantime, my girlfriend had been accepted to the University of Hawaii. We'd been seeing each other for a while and neither of us was looking forward to being apart. We talked things over and decided that we weren't going to be apart, after all. Judy transferred to Cal Poly, majoring in mathematics. Soon we married and in time we would have three beautiful children.

My idea for schooling was to take agronomy courses to give me some education I could take back with me. I could learn something about crop and soil science, plant propagation, and genetics. I wasn't necessarily interested in getting a diploma. I was learning for the sake of learning. I couldn't really see how a diploma would be of much use to me and, in fact, I didn't give the idea of graduation any thought until the end of my third year. I was on a phone call with my mother one day and she said, "So, Raymond, when will you be graduating? Your father and I are really looking forward to it."

Graduating? Was this what my parents were expecting? "In another year, Mom," I managed to reply. Truthfully, I wasn't even close to graduating. My course load had been relatively light, made up of just the agronomy classes that had especially interested me. The next day, I filled my schedule with every course that I could take until I reached the maximum number of credits a student was allowed, and then

I enrolled in night courses for additional credits at nearby Cuesta College. It was a long, grueling year, but I pulled it off. I was able to graduate on time and get my diploma.

I thought about sticking around California, which I had come to love, but couldn't figure out a way to stay in agriculture without working for somebody else, something I didn't want to do. My work on our family farm had been more or less autonomous, and I liked it that way—I liked the independence, the idea that nobody was looking over my shoulder. Judy and I moved back to the Big Island, with her getting a job as a teacher at an elementary and intermediary school. I was offered a teaching position, too, at Honoka'a High School, teaching agriculture, but teaching wasn't for me. Instead, I took a job with the University of Hawaii as a farm extension agent. After a year and a half of that, I determined the job, though good, was not what I wanted to do for the rest of my life. Instead, I came full circle, back to the family farm where I put my education to direct use.

Dad was happy to have me on board and I soon became the farm's operations manager. At the time, our major product was lettuce. We grew various types that we shipped to Oahu on barges owned by a company called Young Brothers. Their ports of call on the Big Island were Hilo and Kawaihae and they ran the barges weekly between those ports and Oahu. These were canopied, open-decked barges towed by big tugboats. The problem was that there was no refrigeration. The trip to Oahu took over a day, and sometimes our lettuce sat in the hot sun for a while before being loaded onto the barges and sometimes it would sit again after being shipped, waiting for the buyer. As a result, what was once high-quality produce ended up being wilted and limp. The wholesalers needed to immediately chill it and then sell it as quickly as possible.

Dad, being a fisherman, understood well the importance of refrigeration. Since the barges had none, he built an insulated container. We'd pre-cool our produce and put it into the container before loading it onto the barges. The container would arrive on Oahu with the temperature holding to within a few degrees, and the wholesaler would now find our produce to be in exceptionally good condition. This system soon encouraged our wholesaler to invest in refrigerated containers. The barges had no electricity, but, along with the other farmers, we'd load our produce into their containers, which would then be chilled to the mid-thirties before being hauled onto the barges. This worked so well that Young Brothers soon began building refrigerated containers. We Big Island farmers were now much more competitive, able to sell quality produce all around the islands. It was a watershed moment for the local agricultural economy.

Nevertheless, we still had a problem. The wholesalers took our products only on consignment. And they paid us what they wanted to pay. We never knew what they were selling our produce for, and, many times, they'd tell us they couldn't sell it at all and had to dump it. The wholesalers held all the cards. The growers had no way of verifying what was really happening with all the produce that was being shipped. Sometimes, a wholesaler would have the

Department of Agriculture inspect the produce and create a memo to send to the farmer declaring that the produce was rotten. This letter might arrive weeks or even a month after shipment, leaving the farmer in the dark in the meantime as to the fate of his shipment. Dad and I tried to convince some of the farmers to organize and agree to sell only FOB the farm, meaning the wholesalers would takes ownership from the point of origin, but other growers rejected the idea, fearful that if you couldn't get all the farmers on board, the rest would be left at a distinct disadvantage.

Eventually, my father and I decided to change the course of our business. We emphasized flowers where we had more control over the selling. We concentrated on our carnations which were still being purchased by the lei makers, and we grew what I believed was a top-of-the-line product. Still, always looking for improvement, I decided to seek a professional opinion and hired a consultant to check out our operation. I chose a farm consultant from Encinitas, California, an area that I knew was known for its flowers. The consultant came out to our farm and looked us over and then recommended that I come see him in California where he would take me around to various Southern California farms. I flew into San Diego with a bunch of our long-stemmed carnations in hand, went to the consultant's office, and took immediate notice of the carnations he had in various vases to test shelf life. The flowers were beautiful and robust and three times the size of ours. I looked around for the nearest trash can into which I dropped my pitiful bunch of carnations.

The consultant said we had the right farm, but we were growing the wrong product. "Roses," he suggested. "Your soil, your cooler climate—you have the perfect conditions to grow roses. That's where your emphasis should be." Roses sounded just fine to me. What's more classic and universally loved than the rose? We quickly switched gears. I knew practically nothing about roses, but I decided to learn all there was to know. If we were going to grow roses, I determined that we were going to do it right.

THREE

Coming Up Roses

I learned quickly that the consultant was right. We did some production trials and enjoyed very positive results, especially with roses we grew in hothouses, which protected the tender buds from temperature fluctuations and disease. The production cycle with our roses turned out to be fast. In fact, it was too fast for the floral demand of the Big Island. Soon, we had more roses than we could sell. We needed to expand our marketplace, and eventually, my sister opened up a wholesale operation on Oahu, selling to the large and more affluent Honolulu market. On Oahu, most roses were imported from the mainland, making them expensive. Some were produced on Oahu, but they were short-stemmed and not the best quality. The long-stemmed premium roses we were growing on the Big Island were soon in high demand and sold quickly.

We sold to a lot of places besides my sister's store, and one memorable buyer was a woman named Emma Kawahara, owner of Emma's Store, a fixture in the heart of Kailua-Kona on the Big Island. Emma sold a lot of tourist items along with candies, beverages, snacks, and a small amount of groceries. Our roses became big sellers there. Emma knew everyone in Kona and everyone knew Emma, including the tourists who stayed around long enough. But for a store owner who dealt with the general public, Emma wasn't exactly the most polite person in the world. She could be coarse and impolite and even downright mean, and if she didn't like how you were acting in her store, she'd have no compunction about asking you to leave and personally escorting you to the door.

I found Emma to be a diamond in the rough. Underneath her brash exterior was a fine person. Her husband was a good guy, too. He came by the farm weekly to buy roses for the store and he'd always ask me to have a drink with him at a local bar. Sometimes this made him late getting back to Kona and he'd get a piece of Emma's mind upon his return, but he always took it in stride. Emma never paid the bill for her roses until I came by her store personally to collect. This meant an hour's drive from the farm each way. I never minded. Emma would insist that we go out to lunch first where she'd give me motherly advice and tell me to watch out for certain people who didn't pay their bills. We'd go back to the store after lunch and she'd fill a grocery bag with food and snacks and hand it to me. I always looked forward to my times with Emma. Every few months, we had our luncheon together and I'd always come back with a check and a bag full of goodies.

Meanwhile, I kept learning all I could about growing roses. I read as many books about rose production as I could lay my hands on. I read articles and talked to other growers. At first, we tried growing different types and colors of roses, figuring that a variety would be the best way to fill the demand. Before long, however, I learned that different colors weren't of interest to the typical Hawaii consumer. Red roses were the dominant sellers by far and so we focused on red, which soon accounted for more than 70 percent of our sales.

We expanded production and I knew I needed to keep learning. I needed to stay current with market trends and I needed to know of the latest in growing technology. I knew that farming techniques were always evolving. I decided to visit with some of the best growers in the world and I began making trips to California, Oregon, British Columbia, New Zealand, France, and the Netherlands. In Amsterdam, they held the annual HortiFair and I'd attend every two or three years. The Fair would attract up to 50,000 professionals every year from over 100 countries. I was amazed by the modern, high-tech greenhouses that the Dutch were using. Holland could be dark and dreary and they needed all the technological help they could get. Despite their climate, they sold some of the best roses in the world, moving two-million dollars' worth of them at wholesale auction every morning.

Of course, the trips weren't all business. There was some fun and sightseeing along the way, too. I took my first trip to Amsterdam with an American contingent of about fifty rose growers. We toured the city and, of course, that meant touring the fabled Red Light District, where ladies of the evening pose in shop windows to attract their customers. We didn't have anything like that in Waimea, let me tell you. Buddies I had made on the trip constantly goaded me to ask one of the girls in the windows as to the going rate for services. Finally, I relented and asked one. "Fifty guilders," she replied. "There," I said to my buddies. "Are you guys happy now?" That's as far as any of us wanted to take things. But back in the hotel bar, I was relaying this story to a Japanese businessman who apparently had more experience in the Red Light District than any of us were looking for. "Fifty?" he said. "Ha! That's where they start. What happens is you go in, then a big guy comes into the room and tells you that you have to pay more!" Thanks for the tip, I told him.

That hotel bar is where I was first introduced to jenever, a juniper-flavored liquor, sometimes known as Dutch gin, made almost exclusively in the Netherlands. Jenever has been around since the 1500s when it was used for medicinal purposes. The bartender insisted I try it, despite my pleas for a simple Scotch rocks. Apparently, there are two kinds of jenever, old (*oude*) and young (*jonge*), each arrived at by a different distilling process. I didn't know this at the time. When I agreed to try jenever, the bartender said, "*Oude* or *jonge*?" I said both.

Touring the city at night, especially the Red Light District, we were told to watch for pickpockets, advice that we all took to heart. Well, of course, there's always a prankster in the group, and ours came up from behind me as we were walking along and grabbed at my wallet. With my heart suddenly racing, I turned and yelled, "Hey!" before I realized who it was. He, of course, thought it was funny until later that evening when he felt a tug from behind on his backpack. Panicking, he grabbed tight to his backpack and began running. Those of us who saw what really happened were doubled over in laughter. His backpack had become snagged on a low tree branch.

After Amsterdam, the group traveled to Cap d'Antibes, in the south of France between Cannes and Nice, to visit with Meilland International, a family-owned rose-growing business founded around 1850 and regarded as one of the best rose growers and breeders in the world. They were nothing less than legends in the industry. We met with Alain Meilland, who was the current head of this rose empire. Most of our commercial varieties came from Meilland's breeding, or inventions, as Alain referred to them. One of the most notable roses that came from years of their complicated crossbreeding was the Peace rose. Francis Meilland cultivated this breed from 1935 to 1939. Anticipating the start of the Second World War, he sent cuttings to friends in Europe and the United States for safekeeping. It is said that the one sent to the US was on the last plane out of France before Germany invaded.

In the US, the Peace rose was cultivated and sent back out into the world where it quickly gained in popularity. It wasn't yet known as the Peace rose, however. That would come at the end of the war when Meilland would ask Field

Marshal Alan Brooke if he could name the rose after him in honor of his role in the liberation of France. Brooke demurred, telling Meilland that nobody would remember his name and that a better, more enduring name would be "Peace." And so it became. In the US, the trade name "Peace" was announced on April 29, 1945, the day Berlin fell to the Allies. And on September 2, 1945, the very day of the formal surrender by the Japanese, the Peace rose was selected as the gold medal winner by the American Rose Society. Later that year, Peace roses were presented to each delegation of the very first meeting of the United Nations in San Francisco. Each rose came with a note: "We hope the Peace rose will influence men's thoughts for everlasting world peace."

Alain Meilland told us the story of the Peace rose and that the Conrad-Pyle Rose Company had received that initial Peace rose from Francis Meilland, the one sent out just before the invasion. Conrad-Pyle did so well with the rose that after the war, the company sent a check to Meilland for 40 million francs in compensation and gratitude. The check saved Meilland International from certain bankruptcy. Francis Meilland then moved the company to Cap d'Antibes from its original location in Tassin, France.

I continued to learn and dedicate myself to producing the best product possible. Our business grew accordingly. Along the way, we had a setback or two. At one point, we were prevented from shipping our roses to Oahu. There was fear of infestation from an insect specific to the Big Island and, for a time, Oahu did not accept any roses from

Big Island farms. That could have been disastrous. To survive, we needed the bigger Oahu market. Fortunately, in the end, we received a certificate from the Department of Agriculture declaring our roses free of the insect and the Oahu market was opened back up to us. We had other minor hiccups from time to time, as any farm does, but our business kept humming along and we expanded. We built more and more greenhouses and ultimately reached a point where we had over 100,000 plants.

We made decent money, but, for me, it wasn't enough. Judy and I had divorced and before long, I knew I needed to send three kids to college. That wasn't going to be cheap. As much as I loved the farm, I took a few years off from it. I knew that real estate on the Big Island at that time was becoming more sought after, and so I opened a real estate business, selling farmland and some residential property. Financially, it proved to be a good move. I did well enough to put my kids through Hawaii Preparatory Academy, and then through university—one to UCLA and two to the University of Hawaii. I was proud of them and gratified that I could give them such great starts. But after their schooling, as good as the real estate money was, I went back to the farm. I'd missed it. And I hadn't cared much for real estate sales, having to deal with the general public and drive people around looking at properties. Deals could go bad for no reason, people could change their minds, financing could fall through—there were a lot of circumstances that always felt beyond my control. In farming, the results had more to do with one's true ability. It was a much better fit for me.

Back on the farm, things rolled along. We cultivated roses, watched the town of Waimea grow around us, and enjoyed the easy-paced lifestyle of Hawaii farming. I had found my place in life.

Then one day, it all threatened to come apart. That damned discoloration, what I had originally blamed on the adjuvant. And it was getting worse. It was most obvious on the bridal pink roses but was soon clearly affecting all of the rose plants. The leaves began to yellow and fall off. The stems were turning brown, too, but it was a slow process, with parts of the stems remaining green. But roses are priced to some degree by the length of the stem and a damaged stem, even just a piece of it, means a drastically less profitable product. Few of the plants actually died although on many, the flowers themselves did. The survivors were greatly inferior to what we were used to growing. Even the scent was affected. It was a nightmare in the making.

I began checking the roots and discovered that they were also getting brown. Additionally, they were significantly weakening. With little effort, you could simply pull the roots out of the ground. By the time we discovered that the problem was the Benlate, some of the plants were hanging onto the soil by just a few fibers. The root damage was especially disconcerting. This suggested a problem that went as deep as the soil. Above-ground damage was one thing. Damage that went below ground was something else. It wasn't just my roses that were dying. My farm was dying, too.

My attorneys informed me that I wasn't alone. Other farms around Hawaii and around the country were dying, too. Dozens at first, and then hundreds. Lawsuits were being filed all over. But DuPont refused to take responsibility and I was forced into a legal fight I never wanted. All I wanted was to have my life back as it had been. All I wanted was to grow my roses.

FOUR

Discoveries

In 1991, DuPont took Benlate off the market. The prevailing belief was that Benlate had accidentally become contaminated during the manufacturing process with an herbicide. They didn't exactly take the product off the market voluntarily; the federal government had to step in. Back in September of 1989, the EPA had issued a temporary stop sale order under the Federal Insecticide, Fungicide, and Rodenticide Act. Then, in March of 1991, they issued a second order. On March 22, DuPont instituted a total recall of Benlate. It was too late. By 1993, more than 2,100 growers across the US were claiming crop damage, damage that cost millions of dollars and tainted thousands of acres of soil.

But DuPont was well positioned for any legal battle thrown at them. What started in 1802 in Wilmington,

Delaware, as a gunpowder mill by French-American chemist Éleuthère Irénée du Pont de Nemours, had grown into a multinational chemical company that would develop such mainstays as nylon, Teflon, Kevlar, Lycra, and Freon. Plus a zillion other chemicals. Their products reached into pretty much every industry and they'd become one of the largest chemical companies in the world. At the time of our trial, DuPont, continuously positioned somewhere in the top half of the Fortune 100 list, had assets of $38 billion, employed 100,000 people, and conducted business in over 100 countries.

During the early years of the Benlate actions, DuPont had an interesting strategy, which would become public later. In a September 1991 letter from the Orlando law firm hired by DuPont to DuPont's legal department, Thomas Burke of Cabaniss and Burke suggested that continued research into the source of contamination was a proper step. So long as the research didn't come to any conclusions, that is. The research would allow DuPont to argue that "it continues to search for a cause." Like a good corporate citizen. Like a company looking out for the welfare of its customers. "It is a much better litigation position to state that we have looked, are looking, and will continue to look but have had no success."[1]

DuPont settled more than $510 million worth of claims, but then stopped in late 1992, asserting that their own research had revealed that Benlate had not, in fact, been contaminated, apparently changing tactics. In fact, what happened, as we would learn, was that their product liability insurance had been exhausted. Up until then, they'd been covered for their losses. But not anymore. Now, facing the prospect of having to make restitution out of their own pocket, their new strategy was to deny.

In August of 1993, while a federal jury deliberated, DuPont settled a consolidated suit that was being tried in Columbus, Georgia for only $4 million and change. That Benlate case, which was the first to go to trial and would set the tone for future cases throughout the country, involved a Georgia nursery business named Bush Ranch, and three other plaintiffs—a farmer in Florida, a farmer in Alabama, and a farmer on Oahu named Warren Kobatake, whom I knew personally. I imagined Warren used the same Benlate I had used. That case had gone to the jury but the settlement took place before the jury had reached a verdict. DuPont representatives called the settlement "a prudent business decision." In fact, DuPont Chairman Edgar S. Woolard Jr. went even further, declaring it "a victory for DuPont, for our employees, and for our science."[2] And indeed it seemed to be. Stan and Andy had been watching the Bush Ranch case closely, even ordering daily court transcripts. The settlement was disappointingly low, a terribly discouraging development. We would learn a lot more about Bush Ranch as our own case proceeded.

Notwithstanding Woolard's proclaimed "victory," there would be more than 500 lawsuits filed against DuPont throughout the country by 1994, including dozens in Hawaii. These suits revealed internal DuPont documentation that pointed the finger at numerous toxic contaminants, the deadliest of which was sulfonylurea, a highly potent weed killer that was made at the same Belle, West Virginia plant where benomyl, the chief ingredient in Benlate was also made. Cross contamination seemed the likely culprit. But DuPont's position was that this documentation was being taken "out of context." Apparently, there had been a memo that referenced not sulfonylurea, but atrazine, a far less potent herbicide. Either way, DuPont continued to insist that there had been no contamination.[3] Their Benlate had been just fine. In fact, in the Bush Ranch case, they had brought in representatives from Alta Analytical Laboratory, an independent lab out of California, to testify that they'd found no sulfonylureas at any of the four farms involved in the suit.

Nevertheless, on a single day in April of 1994, DuPont would settle 220 of their pending lawsuits, including sixty in Hawaii, paying out $214 million, all while continuing to maintain their product was not responsible for the damage being claimed. The plaintiffs agreed to the settlement based primarily on the Bush Ranch case, figuring that was as good as they were going to get. None wanted to risk taking their cases any further. For DuPont's part, a company spokesperson said the 220 settlements would have no effect on any remaining suits. "We have no plans to negotiate on any of them," the spokesperson claimed.[4] And yet, as time went along, they continued to settle. They even settled with other Hawaii farmers.

But not with us.

I felt from the start that Stan and Andy were the right guys to take the case. Their firm was probably the most recognized one in Hilo. Stan Roehrig was a bulldog, a take-no-prisoners guy, and the bad cop to Andy's good cop. And as smart as they came. Born and raised in Hawaii, Stan had graduated from Brown University with a degree in physics before getting his law degree from the University of Washington School of Law in Seattle in June of 1965. He moved back to Hawaii with his fiancé and served as a public defender in Hilo, then as a member of the State House of Representatives for eight years as chairman of the agriculture and judiciary committees. Finally, he settled into private practice.

Andy Wilson was one of the founding partners in Stan's law firm. Born and raised in Hilo, he was, like me, an alum of Cal State Poly. He earned his law degree from the University of San Diego School of Law before returning to Hilo where he served as a deputy prosecuting attorney before going into practice with Stan. His style was softer than Stan's, perhaps a little more analytical. Each served as an effective counterpart to the other. Together, they made a terrific team.

Right off the bat, Stan and Andy dug in, researching all the other cases around the country. In fact, early on in the process, the plaintiffs' attorneys in all the other DuPont cases had gotten together in Orlando, Florida for a three-day weekend to share information in a kind of "plaintiffs against DuPont" convention. Stan and Andy attended, taking with them a young attorney they had just hired, Kris LaGuire, who would become the third man on our legal team. There were probably thirty attorneys at the gathering representing farmers mostly from Georgia, Florida, California, the Caribbean, and a handful of us from Hawaii. It was in the more tropical climates where Benlate had been used most, owing to the fact that the tropical moisture was what required the need for a plant fungicide in the first place. Stan and Andy had already been in phone contact with a lot of these guys, so there was a certain amount of familiarity by the time they met. The meeting went well. It was a group of "swashbuckling" plaintiffs' attorneys, as Stan referred to them, and besides the branch of law they practiced, they all had one critical thing in common: they were all going up against a giant in DuPont. They were all underdogs. The attendees all felt a shared bond and Stan, Andy, and Kris came back even more emboldened. Some of the friendships forged in Orlando would last for years.

The deal between me and the firm of Roehrig Wilson was simple: they'd work on the standard contingency of one-third, but I was responsible for paying the out-of-pocket costs—research, travel, long-distance phone calls, even photocopies. I assumed these costs would be significant but not crushing, maybe a few thousand bucks. I was still hoping for a settlement. I was still looking for the $80,000 I'd calculated. I imagined the whole thing would be over in a couple of months, maybe even less. A couple of strongly worded letters and a phone call or two and I'd be on my way.

A few thousand bucks? In time, my costs would run beyond thousands. My costs would run into the millions. An additional attorney would be needed—Steve Cox, an outstanding litigator from San Francisco who, by then, had settled a Benlate case for a Maui grower. A staff of assistants would be required, too. When the trial would finally commence in Kona, condos would need to be rented for my legal team for living quarters and office space. The photocopies? That seemingly insignificant expense would run over $100,000.

But all of that was ahead of me. In the meantime, Stan and Andy had taken on another DuPont case, filing suit for a fellow farmer and friend of mine, Stanley Tomono. Stanley had started his farm in 1972 after returning from military service in Vietnam where he'd received a Bronze Star for bravery and two Purple Hearts for combat injuries. Stanley grew cucumbers and tomatoes and quickly became one of the largest growers in the state. He grew orchids, too, starting with 1,800 plants and, by 1991, growing his inventory to 2.5 million. But Benlate had destroyed his crops just like they had destroyed mine. His cucumber production dropped from 1,400 cases a week to 200. His orchid production fell from forty bags of flowers a day to ten. His farm, like mine, was dying a slow death. I got in touch with Stanley and suggested we join forces. He agreed.

With Tomono on board, Andy and Stan brought in experts—chemists, agronomists, economists. It was quickly determined that my damages had grown substantially. The case would be filed for much, much more than $80,000. There were extenuating circumstances. The contaminant was affecting my roses, my soil, and even the buildings. It wasn't a question of simply losing a season—or even two or three seasons—of crops. The loss would be an ongoing one. I could see it happening even as we prepared for the suit. My production was steadily decreasing and there didn't seem to be a bottom. How long could I keep the farm going? How long before I'd have to sell? And even then, what's a farm worth with contaminated soil? Any kind of long-term solution would require restoration and rebuilding to get my farm back to the way it was before my use of Benlate. It would be as though I'd need to completely scrub clean my farm and start anew.

The experts Stan and Andy brought in determined the damages like so: economic loss, $2,635,347; soil restoration, $1,351,084; and farm structure damages, $9,303,055. Total damages: $13,289,486. Because of the size of Tomono's farm, his damages were even greater: roughly $29 million. The time for DuPont to get off cheaply was over. By refusing to settle for the initial damages I had claimed at the start, they had brought upon themselves a full-fledged war. Why? To this day, I wonder at the thought process. Part of it might be that Tomono and I were small-town farmers on a rural island 2,000 miles away from the mainland. Maybe they were hoping we would simply go away, that we and our small-town lawyers would crumble in the face of their big, corporate intimidation. But because they settled with other Hawaii growers, I'm inclined to believe that perhaps there was another reason. Stan and Andy were instrumental in helping other plaintiffs' attorneys around the country against DuPont, just as those plaintiffs' attorneys were instrumental in helping Stan and Andy. Surely, DuPont had learned of those Orlando conferences. They knew of the growing network of attorneys that were suing them. It might just be that DuPont wanted to send a message, to break up the league of attorneys. Or, by playing hardball with us, to at least get the other farmers to agree to settle their pending cases. I suspect that DuPont gave their lawyers a blank check to make this happen, figuring one major stand would be worth whatever the cost. Defense attorneys dream of such clients. In reality, DuPont wasn't interested in simply defending themselves. They were interested in pummeling us to the ground as an example to everybody else.

Their tactics became clear during the discovery phase of the suit. This is where each side gets to see what the other side's evidence is so neither should be blindsided by surprise evidence in the middle of the trial. Contrary to the movies and TV court dramas, surprise witnesses rarely pop up at the end of the trial to turn the case on its head. In our case, the discovery process included a lot of depositions—questioning under oath by witnesses for both sides of the suit. The chemists, agronomists, and economists were all deposed. These would become expert witnesses. My workers were all deposed. Naturally, I was deposed and my deposition lasted for two long days.

More than anything else, however, the discovery process in our case hinged on documentation. DuPont had internal memos implying they knew a lot more about the contamination than they were letting on. They had reports from analyses they'd done, statements regarding their own evaluations. In fact, with all the suits that had been filed, there was so much documentation that DuPont had opened a central depository at their headquarters in Wilmington to warehouse it all. At first, they demanded that my attorneys travel there to retrieve what they wanted. Stan told the judge assigned to our case, Judge Ronald Ibarra, that this was unreasonable and Ibarra agreed, forcing DuPont to send the documentation to Hilo. But the cost had to be borne by our side, which is what DuPont really wanted. They knew who was paying the bills. Their hope was to bleed me and Stanley Tomono dry before the trial even started.

It was about this time that Steve Cox from San Francisco came aboard. His previous experience with the Maui Benlate case would become invaluable to us. He was there when the documents started coming in and was able to analyze and make sense of them. And he knew how to question the experts.

Our requests for DuPont's relevant documentation went on for more than a year before the trial, with Andy and Stan and the DuPont attorneys meeting once a week in front of Judge Ibarra to hash the requests out. It became a standing appointment. Not surprisingly, DuPont was reluctant to turn over documents that might have shown problems with Benlate, thus beginning a long process of foot-dragging that would end up being one of the most significant hallmarks of the case. Steve called it the coffee-drip method of producing documents. Repeatedly, my attorneys had to file "motions to compel," basically asking the judge to force DuPont to properly and fully respond to the requests. The level of DuPont's stonewalling was such that from the commencement of the discovery process in November of 1992, through the trial, and even post-trial, the judge would issue fifty-four discovery orders against them, twenty-seven of which would result in sanctions—monetary penalties assessed by calculating the additional amount of time and effort our side had to expend to ultimately get what we had asked for in the first place. Sanctions from before the trial alone totaled over $200,000. The problem is, sanctions aren't paid right away. It's not like DuPont had to write a check each time they got sanctioned by Judge Ibarra. The sanction amounts get totaled up and reconciled later, at the very conclusion of the case. And so, given the information that was in those documents, it was worth it to DuPont to just let the sanctions accrue, figuring it would be a small price to pay down the road if they won the case. And besides, what was $200,000 to DuPont?

When they did turn over documents, they turned them over by the thousands. They came in banker's boxes—heavy storage file boxes that were at least two feet deep and fifteen inches wide each. On one day alone, they delivered forty of them. Down the road, Judge Ibarra, handing out yet one more sanction to DuPont, would criticize them for this "dump truck discovery," as he called it. The strategy, of course, was to force my attorneys to have to go through each box file by file to find the one needle-in-a-haystack document they were looking for. It was just more time and effort that had to be expended.

And over time, the boxes kept coming. Andy and Stan had to rent out an empty office across the hallway from their offices in Hilo just to have a place to put them all. The boxes were stacked up to the ceiling with narrow pathways between them just wide enough for a person to fit through. It was grueling and arduous, but little by little, they whittled down the documents and files to a number that fit into five of the banker's boxes. Then, they whittled the documents down to three boxes. Finally, one box. Stan called it the "hot docs box." With the hot docs box, Stan and Andy had what they felt they needed to go to trial.

Even still, DuPont tried to stifle the evidence by claiming some of the documentation was subject to what's called work–product privilege. It's a bit like attorney–client privilege, wherein certain evidence that you put together on your own side's behalf to go to trial is considered confidential and not for public view. DuPont claimed that a lot of their documentation came under this privilege. Judge Ibarra brought in two retired judges to act as discovery masters. Masters are charged with reviewing evidence in cases where there's a lot of it, thus alleviating the judge from having to rule on every scrap of paper and, theoretically, speeding the discovery process along. The masters determined that every document out of those banker boxes, but maybe eight or ten, should be disclosed to us. According to the masters, DuPont's claims of work–product privilege were not legally sufficient, and they recommended that the documents be produced. Judge Ibarra ordered DuPont to do so. Three times, DuPont filed appeals to the Hawaii Supreme Court seeking to reverse Ibarra's decisions. DuPont lost all three times.

Long after the trial, Stan would learn from one of the attorneys with the firm who represented DuPont locally that DuPont's main team of lawyers on the mainland had employed psychologists to help with pretrial strategy. Apparently, the idea was to get into the heads of Stan and Andy, to proceed in the ways that would most intimidate them or get them emotionally involved to the point where they wouldn't make smart decisions. DuPont wanted to psyche my attorneys out, as if it were a prize fight and not a civil trial. They knew all the tricks and were probably inventing new ones every day.

For our side, we managed to keep some of DuPont's evidence out of the trial. There was a neighboring farm that used Benlate and it was DuPont's idea to use the results of soil testing on that farm to show that there had been no contamination. I knew the results were suspect. Watanabe Farms had opened on the Big Island because I wouldn't sell my roses to their wholesale flower business on Oahu. I had tried, but they would allow me to sell to them only on consignment, just like the produce wholesalers. I had refused. But Watanabe liked my roses and so they decided to start growing their own on the Big Island, buying a vacant farm next to me. They had become a competitor, in other words. Worse, their general manager had left them to come work for me. The bottom line was that they didn't care very much for Kawamata Farms and they had no reservations about giving DuPont access to their soil and even testifying on DuPont's behalf, if asked. For all I knew, DuPont was probably planning on paying them. Handsomely, no doubt.

Ultimately, the judge decided that the results of the trials that Watanabe conducted on their rose farm to be used against us would be irrelevant and Watanabe never became a factor. Nevertheless, it was disheartening to think a fellow grower, indeed a neighbor, would side with DuPont, even if they were a competitor. Yes, farming could be a competitive industry, like any other, but there's always been a kind of unwritten code based on mutual respect. Farmers help each other. So do neighbors.

We got another break during the discovery process, and it was a big one. Stan and Andy did some research into that Belle, West Virginia DuPont plant where both the Benlate and the weed killers were made. Belle was a DuPont company town. The high school, in fact, was "DuPont High." Stan and Andy found an expert, a professor at an East Coast university, to go to the plant and examine it for cross contamination, to see if he could find evidence that the Belle plant was, in fact, the reason that herbicides had been found in my soil, despite the fact that I'd never used them. Naturally, DuPont fought against the professor's inspection. Judge Ibarra compelled DuPont to allow the professor access but, even then, there were parts of the plant DuPont refused to allow the professor into. Stan and Andy had to file another motion to compel and the professor was able to go back a second time to inspect the previously closed off areas, finding that cross contamination was indeed a problem at the Belle plant.

But then Stan and Andy did one better. Through a West Virginia attorney, they found an employee who would be willing to testify about the cross contamination at the plant. The lawyer had been representing other DuPont employees who had contracted cancer and other health problems, presumably from the chemicals at the Belle plant. There was a significant history of illness in the town. But such was the level of loyalty to DuPont in Belle that some of the employees who had sued DuPont had faced harassment from townspeople—even threats and acts of vandalism. DuPont had represented the livelihoods of so many of the residents of Belle that, even in the face of disproportionate rates of cancer, those residents had seemingly banded together to defend their employer. But this one employee, a sixty-year-old former forklift operator suffering from cancer himself, agreed to fly out to Hilo to have his testimony videotaped even though he'd never flown before. Several DuPont employees showed up at the West Virginia airport and badgered and bullied him, but he stood his ground and got on the plane.

The man arrived wearing jeans, suspenders, and a flannel shirt and sat in Stan and Andy's conference room, questioned by Stan, Andy, and DuPont's attorneys, who had flown over from Honolulu that morning. Now the badgering came from DuPont's attorneys, but under questioning from my guys, the man testified to the fact that the same forklift was used in both sections of the plant. Cross contamination was not only possible, it was likely. Try as they might, the DuPont attorneys couldn't shake his testimony. Later, during the trial, his testimony would be played for the jury and would be a significant factor in the outcome.

The man was scheduled to fly back the day after his deposition, but that evening, after the man had returned to his hotel room, my attorneys began thinking that DuPont's guys could conceivably subpoena him for trial, forcing him to either stick around for the trial or have to come all the way back. The trial was still weeks away. He couldn't stay that long and there was no guarantee he'd return, especially with the state of his health, thus potentially nullifying his testimony. But to subpoena him, DuPont's attorneys would have had to do it while he was still on the Island. Taking no chances, Kris LaGuire was dispatched to pick the man up at his hotel and whisk him immediately to the airport, putting him on the very next plane out of Hilo. Understanding what was at stake, the man was more than willing to comply. He trusted DuPont even less than we did and I think he was happy to leave and have the whole matter behind him.

I was more than a little suspicious of DuPont's tricks. While all the pretrial stuff was playing out, Tomono and I had dozens of meetings with Stan and Andy. I was on the phone with one of them at least daily. Maybe I had watched too many movies based on John Grisham thrillers of corporate and legal espionage, but I couldn't help but wonder if DuPont, as big as they were, might be willing to skirt a few rules and engage in tactics that included bugging our phones. I knew that with each lawsuit filed, their stock was dropping. There were millions upon millions of dollars at stake. The top brass was under enormous pressure. Would they become desperate? Would they cross the line of legality?

My sister, employed by the phone company at the time, did nothing to temper my concern. "Oh, yes," she said, "it's absolutely possible to tap a line. It's really pretty easy." I spoke freely to my attorneys in the privacy of their offices, but I was very careful on the phone. Stan and Andy both encouraged my cautiousness. In this age before cell phones, Stan and I both had radiotelephones and we often conversed over those. I didn't imagine there were more than twenty other radiotelephones on the whole island. Even still, we were careful not to mention specifics about the trial. I knew that radiotelephones could be scanned and so we spoke in generalities only, leaving the details for our face-to-face meetings.

The days dragged on and the time and energy it was taking to have the case put together was almost overwhelming. It was frustrating and demanding, far more so than I could have imagined. And then, with the trial just a few weeks away, DuPont made a motion that threatened to undo all the work my attorneys had done. Leaving no stone unturned, DuPont's attorneys got wind that a new associate at Roehrig Wilson had once clerked for Judge Ibarra. The associate had nothing to do with our case, but DuPont claimed conflict of interest and moved to disqualify our law firm. In a flash, I saw our case going out the window. Would I have to start all over again with another law firm? Who would I find and how quickly could they get up to speed? Most importantly, how much would it cost me? Naturally, that last concern was what DuPont was counting on, that the cost would be prohibitive and Tomono and I would simply drop it. A hearing was held on the matter in front of a Hilo judge and, fortunately, it was decided that Stan and Andy could continue as my attorneys. I breathed a sigh of relief. I was going to get my day in court after all. Little did I know how long that day would last.

FIVE

David v. Goliath

The courthouse in Kona wasn't technically in Kona. It was in nearby Kealakekua, all lush and green and high up to where you can look down at the tropical coastline. The locale brought to mind the old song "My Little Grass Shack in Kealakekua, Hawaii." The courthouse, in fact, wasn't much more than that. The building started out not as a courthouse but as a small hospital and it served in that capacity until a new hospital was built for the town. Parking spaces were scarce, the lobby was small, and the courtroom was cramped. The jury room was actually outside the courtroom, forcing the jurors to walk past the lawyers and pocket-sized gallery during their breaks. The law library was where the hospital morgue used to be and law clerks sometimes reported lights mysteriously flickering on and off. At any rate, in 1994, that's where our trial began in front of Judge Ronald Ibarra, a local, born not just in Kona, but, remarkably, in the old hospital itself, the very site of the courtroom he was now presiding over. (Years after our trial, in October of 2019, Judge Ibarra himself would deliver a grand-opening speech in front of a beautiful new Kona courthouse.)

Judge Ibarra was well respected and known for being tough but fair. That's what Andy and Stan both said about him and they were pleased that he was appointed to hear the case. His background certainly seemed to favor us. He grew up on a nearby coffee farm and was just the kind of local, small-town, farm-friendly person we would have selected ourselves if the choice would have been up to us. Maybe we could hope for a little sympathy.

Ibarra's father immigrated from the Philippines with just a second-grade education. His mother, who had only gone as far as eighth grade, impressed upon young Ronald the importance of school. Upon graduation from Konawaena High, he went to the University of Hawaii, graduating as a second lieutenant through the university's ROTC program. After serving in Colorado and then Thailand, he came back home to Kona where he found work at the Sheraton as a dishwasher and eventually a manager. But he wanted to do something more with his life and he decided to try law, enrolling in the law school at Santa Clara University in California.

There, Ibarra found his calling. He traveled east after graduating and earned a second law degree at Georgetown, thinking he might like to someday teach law. Then he came back home again, first working for the prosecutor's office and then working for a private law firm. He did a stint as managing director for the mayor at one point, too, and then eventually went back to the prosecutor's office. Finally, in 1989, five years before our trial, Ibarra was appointed as a circuit judge in Kona.

Now, the forty-six-year-old judge was about to hear what would be one of the biggest cases of his judicial career, before or since. But any idea I'd had that his Hawaiian roots as the son of a farmer would cause him to sympathize with us were quickly dispelled by the way he handled the courtroom. Stan and Andy were right that he was tough. I would witness, from the start and throughout the trial, that Ibarra didn't have much patience for lawyerly tactics that bordered on the underhanded or for anything he felt was a time waster. He was quick to admonish the attorneys and he was just as quick to admonish our side as theirs.

In fact, it seemed to me that Ibarra came down harder on Stan Roehrig than on anyone else, almost as if he were trying to prove his impartiality. Then again, I noticed Stan was a little more aggressive than the other attorneys, a little more vigorous. Ibarra wanted to make sure he didn't cross any lines of procedure or decorum. Stan was often demonstrative and moved his hands around a lot. He had a tendency to sort of drift around when he was in front of the courtroom and if he got too close to the bench or the witness stand, Ibarra wasn't shy about telling him to take a step back. Nonetheless, I would notice throughout the course of the trial that on the days when Ibarra would come down on Stan the hardest, those would also be the days we could expect some kind of favorable ruling about some unresolved trial issue. Maybe there was a connection, maybe not, but Stan would get admonished and I'd think, "This is going to end up being a good day for us."

The parties to the trial were many and you almost needed a program to keep them straight. Stanley Tomono and I, represented by Stan Roehrig and Andy Wilson (joined by Kris LaGuire and Steve Cox), were suing both DuPont, the manufacturer, and United Agri Products, the distributor. But the suit against DuPont included two other defendants—Platte Chemical Co. and Bartlo Packaging, Inc. Our position was that both of these companies were at least partly responsible for the end product from DuPont. The suit against United Agri included Loveland Industries, their subsidiary, as well as United Agri Products Hawaii, the local company in Hilo where Tomono and I had purchased Benlate. Additionally, we were suing Terra International, Inc., another packaging company.

Now, all these could have been separate court cases, but Judge Ibarra made a decision to consolidate them for discovery purposes. In fact, Judge Ibarra consolidated the discovery for all of the DuPont cases taking place on the Big Island. This way, a dozen different plaintiffs' attorneys wouldn't have to file a dozen different motions for the same DuPont document. By the time we got to court, however, those other Hawaii cases had been settled. Each and every one had been settled, in fact, but ours.

For DuPont's part, they brought a legal staff from their corporate offices, but for representation in Hawaii, they needed lawyers licensed to practice in the state. For that, they hired a large Honolulu law firm—Goodsill, Anderson, Quinn, and Stifel, one of the most known firms around. In turn, the firm sent three of their best—John Lacy, Lisa Munger, and Bruce Lamon. Lacy would be more or less the front person who would give the opening statement and closing argument, and examine most of the witnesses. Lacy was an older guy with a big build, white hair, and mustache. Like all of DuPont's representatives, he came across as polished and wore expensive suits. Munger would examine witnesses, too, particularly the scientific experts, but be more behind the scenes than Lacy. Quickly, we could see that she was the brains of the group, the quarterback of the team, focused on strategy and planning. Lamon was younger and seemed to be more of an assistant to the others.

United Agri was represented by Calvin Young of Libkuman, Ventura, Ayabe, Chong, and Nishimoto. Terra International was represented by David Gruebner of Burke, Sakai, McPheeters, and Bordner. Both law firms, like DuPont's, were based in Honolulu. But it was clear to all that DuPont was running the show. Every day, our side would have two lawyers present in the courtroom, with the other half of the foursome busy preparing or doing research. The opposition never seemed to have less than five attorneys in the courtroom and sometimes as many as ten. If the decision would have been made based on the amount of legal representation, Ibarra would have stopped the trial before it even started and awarded the victory to DuPont. And all of DuPont's attorneys were polished and well-dressed, like Lacy. Not that my attorneys didn't look the part. My understanding, however, is that Stan Roehrig needed a little prompting in the wardrobe department. Outside of court, his typical dress was jeans, docksiders, and a surfing T-shirt. For court, left to his own devices, it would have been a blue blazer, khaki pants, and docksiders every single day. Fortunately for our side, his wife took him clothes shopping before the trial began and enhanced his wardrobe a little.

Leading up to the trial, there were still a lot of motions being filed. For one thing, we were still seeking documentation that DuPont was refusing to turn over. For DuPont's part, they made a motion to have the case summarily dismissed, although that's almost obligatory for a defendant in any trial. Their particular argument was that their responsibility only extended so far. There was a "limitation of liability" provision in the warranty on the Benlate label. Ibarra denied the motion, ruling that their warranty disclaimers and limitation of remedies provisions were "unconscionable." Just because you put something on a label, it doesn't release you from liability. Other motions filed by both sides involved various pieces of evidence—what could be introduced to the jury and what could not.

Finally, on June 14, 1994, the trial began. The first step in a jury trial is choosing the jury, known in the legal profession as *voir dire*. And it's anything but easy. For a fair trial, you need impartial, disinterested, unprejudiced people. But how many people do you know who don't have some kind of opinion about justice? Everyone brings to the table their own presuppositions. DuPont needed to find people who didn't have some kind of bias against big business. For us, we knew that a juror who was sympathetic to local farmers and businesses could be an advantage. Then again, would a Big Island juror, looking at the amount of money we were asking for, feel some resentment? If the trial went in our favor, we'd get a big payday and they'd have to go home to their life of hard work. A lot of factors played into the selection process and it was easy to overanalyze.

At one point, Stan made a motion objecting to the fact that DuPont was running ads on local TV about their famous product Teflon. Well, of course, these were just normal commercials that were being shown nationally, but Stan made the point that they could influence a jury member and that DuPont should be prevented from running them. A good trial lawyer has to try everything, I guess, but Judge Ibarra flatly denied the motion, telling Stan that he was free to ask any potential juror about the ads if he wanted to, but that he wasn't about to force DuPont to change or stop their nationwide television campaign.

Their side made a bit of a misstep right off the bat; John Lacy asked the potential jurors if any of them were acquainted with Stanley Tomono "from Napo'opo'o," only he terribly mispronounced it as *Napopo*. I noticed some of the potential jurors chuckling. It was a small thing, but when you put it with the expensive suit, I knew it didn't play well with the people who were going to decide the case. Lacy was clearly an outsider.

The potential jurors were questioned by both sides and each side was allowed three peremptory challenges. A peremptory challenge means you can reject a potential juror without cause. Maybe you don't like the look on his or her face. Maybe you don't like the way they dress. Maybe they're uneducated. Maybe they're too educated. It seemed to me that a lot of it was done on gut feel. Stan and Andy allowed Tomono and me to confer with them on each juror, happy to enlist our opinions. We all put our heads together and tried to decide whether any given juror gave us a better chance or a worse chance.

When you're out of peremptory challenges, you can still ask that any potential juror be excluded, but you have to have reasonable cause. If, for example, we had discovered that a potential juror worked for DuPont, we could have objected and it wouldn't have cost us one of the three peremptory challenges. The judge has to determine the validity of the objection, however. He has final say. He gets involved in the questioning of the potential jurors, too. Among other standard questions, Ibarra would always ask if any of the jury candidates knew any of the lawyers, plaintiffs, or defendants. One potential juror said, "Yes, I know Stan Roehrig."

"How do you know him?" Ibarra asked.

"He's my surfing buddy. We surf together at Honoli'i," the man replied.

Ibarra asked for clarification. "You go surfing together? You go to Honoli'i *with* Mr. Roehrig?"

"No, no, I just see him there."

"When do you see him there?"

"I see him when the waves are big."

It was clear that the two were acquaintances at most. Stan confirmed this in a sidebar. "He's not my *buddy*," Stan insisted. Nevertheless, Ibarra dismissed the man. That was just Ibarra being fair.

Both sides used up their peremptory challenges in pretty short order and a number of objections were made as well. Twelve jurors needed to be selected and the questioning was long and intense. One of the final potential jurors questioned was a man named Nathan Yamada who mentioned that he loved the outdoors. He loved the water and would frequently go spearfishing. He complained about an underwater fishing hole he used to visit. It had become polluted with what he believed was Clorox. He believed it would take years for the fish to come back. It was a different kind of chemical contamination than ours, but contamination nevertheless. Ibarra asked Yamada if he thought he could be neutral in the case. "Yes, Your Honor," he said. Ibarra approved him for the jury, a potential victory for our side.

Not until June 29 was the full jury of twelve sworn in, with an additional three as alternates. It had been two weeks of full days; nine in the morning until four in the afternoon. I don't imagine it takes two weeks to complete most trials, let alone jury selection. That should have been a sign. One of the questions Ibarra had asked the members of the jury was whether they could commit themselves to a trial that might take as long as two to three months. Little did any of us know how long this trial would really drag out.

Finally, the opening statements began. Stan made ours. He came across as self-assured, if not a bit brash, and I could sense the jury liked him right away. Essentially, he argued that the Benlate had been contaminated with sulfonylureas and other plant killers when DuPont manufactured it, and, because of these defects, Benlate caused our crop damage.

In the course of presenting our side, Stan mentioned another case involving Benlate, a very similar case, in which DuPont lost. Immediately, John Lacy stood up for DuPont and objected, arguing that the revelation was prejudicial. Ibarra asked both attorneys to approach the bench where Lacy asked for a mistrial. A mistrial would mean that the jury we had just spent two weeks selecting would be discharged, and our trial would have to be rescheduled with a new jury. It would mean more expense and more time. Ibarra told the jury to retire to the jury room. Everyone waited while they walked through the courtroom past the counsel tables and small gallery to the exit, and then both sides argued the relevance of the other Benlate case. Again, I had visions of everything we had worked so hard on going down the drain. Finally, Ibarra said he'd rule on Lacy's motion for a mistrial, but that in the meantime, he'd allow the case to continue. The jury was brought back in and Stan resumed his opening statement.

The next day, Ibarra ruled against Lacy. The trial would continue. This was a relief, but also a revelation to me of what was to come. Both sides had very smart people well-versed in the law, experienced in the courtroom, and always looking for some technicality or other upon which to pounce. But as smart as our guys were, I worried about the skill of the other side. DuPont's deep pockets meant they could afford the very best representation. The difference in resources was clear. Andy and Stan, with the help of Kris LaGuire and Steve Cox, did a lot of their own grunt work. DuPont's team had staffs of people. During lunch breaks, their staff members would be doing research and putting together exhibits and whatever else needed doing, while the attorneys headed out to nice restaurants. For our part, we'd gather in the court library—the old morgue—and eat take-out for lunch with Stan and Andy explaining to us the nuances of the trial and preparing their strategies for the afternoon. In the evenings, if I didn't travel back to Waimea, we'd all meet in one of the small condos the law firm rented (at our expense), and someone would go out to the grocery store and bring back some precooked dinners. The next day, I'd overhear DuPont's attorneys talking about which fine dining establishment they'd visited (at DuPont's expense) and the expensive bottles of wine they'd ordered.

Stan referred to their side as *ton-ton-tons*, a name he coined from the Saturday matinees he remembered attending as a kid for ten cents. A lot of these were serial movies, mostly westerns, and at the end of each one, the good guys always got themselves into a jam that looked hopeless. The big, bad guys would get the upper hand. And right before the caption came up that said, "To be continued," you'd always hear the same three ominous musical notes, the second a half note lower than the first, and then the third bottoming out and holding for a few extra beats: *ton ton TONNN...*

Dupont had the big, bad guys. They were the *ton-ton-tons*. Me, I thought in more Biblical metaphors. As the trial proceeded, I couldn't shake the feeling that our side was David and their side was Goliath. And I knew that outside of the Bible and maybe serial westerns, David rarely wins.

SIX

The Tricks of the Trade

I expected the trial might be lengthy. A month, maybe. Perhaps even two. That expectation seems, in hindsight, magnificently naïve. The trial dragged through the rest of 1994 and on into 1995, *seven months* in all. All those chemists and agronomists and economists that Stan and Andy had brought in were called to the stand as witnesses. One was the professor they had sent to the Benlate plant in West Virginia who testified that he had found evidence of cross contamination. Of course the videotaped testimony of the forklift driver was played, too. DuPont, of course, had their own share of witnesses, a steady stream of them. In total, fifty-five witnesses would be called to the stand. It was day after day after day of direct examination, cross-examination, and redirect. Some of it, after almost thirty years, is hazy. Some of it seems like yesterday.

So it is with my memories of my own testimony. Some of it clear, some of it muddled. I was on the stand for two days and the one thing I clearly remember was John Lacy's manner of questioning. He was tough and relentless, and I just kept hoping his questions would end and I could be excused from the stand. Lacy went for the kill, trying continuously to catch me in an inconsistent answer to something. At one point, he asked why I had stopped taking soil samples on my farm. Taking soil samples was routine for me. I would send the samples out to a lab to determine if my soil was nutrient-deficient in some way or what fertilizer I should add. But when the legal action began, I decided to stop taking samples. Truthfully, I was afraid that maybe the lab would discover that I was doing something wrong. There was no doubt that DuPont's product was the source of my plant damage, but I didn't want anything muddying the waters. I didn't want DuPont to have some other issue they could point to as at least partially responsible for the decreased production of my rose plants.

Lacy drilled me about this. "Why didn't you continue taking soil samples, Mr. Kawamata?" he asked.

I didn't know how to answer and heard myself saying, "I got busy."

"Busy?" Lacy pressed. "What were you so busy doing, Mr. Kawamata?"

"I was courting my wife," I replied. It was true, at least partly. At the time, I had begun dating my second wife,

Joanne, and we'd spent a lot of time together. The jury found it amusing and laughed, and I guess Lacy figured there was nothing more he was going to get out of me. "No more questions," he said.

I was also questioned by Calvin Young, one of the attorneys representing United Agri. I had met Calvin back in the early days of my legal action, back when I'd first hired my lawyers, when I was still willing to settle for that original $80,000. Back then, things weren't so contentious and I'd actually become friends with Calvin. In fact, during the early part of the trial, we even went out to dinner a few times, something Calvin warned me to never reveal to Stan or Andy. Especially Stan. "He'd throw a fit if he knew you were having dinner with the opposition," he said. Calvin would bring along David Gruebner, a young attorney representing Terra International. We all made it a point never to discuss the trial. It was just three guys having dinner and drinks and enjoying some laughs. Once, I joked, "Hey, go easy on me when I'm up on the stand," and, maybe it was just coincidence, but when Calvin questioned me, it was brief and of little consequence. I came to understand the defense attorneys were just regular guys doing their jobs, just like Stan and Andy were doing theirs.

I felt that way about the local guys, anyway. But I never got a warm feeling about the contingent of DuPont attorneys. They seemed cold and calculating, almost machine-like, and always looking for an edge, a way to take advantage somehow. In fact, my other clear recollections are of the unscrupulous tactics they used. I imagine these stood out to me because, at the time, I was still laboring under the misapprehension that inside an American court of law, everyone was bound and determined to play by the rules. I assumed there was a level of honor, some sort of code that attorneys—officers of the court, no less—always followed. I found myself continually surprised and disappointed by DuPont's lawyers.

Case in point: Lacy was ruthless when he had Stanley Tomono on the stand, badgering him and at one point even bringing up a simple mistake he had made on a tax return one year. "Isn't it true that you misled the Internal Revenue Service?" Lacy accused. "Isn't it? Isn't it a fact that you *lied* to them, Mr. Tomono?" Stanley's eyes welled up with tears at the interrogation and I wondered how a guy like Lacy could sleep at night.

That hadn't been the first example I'd seen of John Lacy's underhandedness. Early in the trial, he questioned Alan Teshima, the DuPont representative from Oahu who had tested my farm's soil. Subsequently, he had delivered a memo stating that he'd discovered the presence of atrazine. On the witness stand, he not only denied that he'd discovered atrazine, he denied the existence of the memo. He didn't get very far. We presented the memo as evidence and he had to recant his testimony. It was hard for me to be upset specifically with Teshima because I had the sense that DuPont was telling him how to answer the questions on the stand. I figured he was just trying to be a good soldier, trying to hold onto his job. In fact, we discovered that he had not only been coached on what to say beforehand, he was coached during his actual testimony.

Tomono noticed it first. He nudged me with his elbow while Teshima was on the stand and whispered, "Watch Lacy."

"Why?"

"After he asks a question. When he nods his head downward, Teshima answers yes. When he nods his head to the side, he answers no. He's doing it on almost every question."

I watched for the next ten or fifteen minutes and saw that Tomono was right. Lacy was clearly signaling what he wanted the answers to be. Now, neither Tomono nor I knew this was necessarily improper. We weren't lawyers, after all. We didn't know the rules of a courtroom. Tomono whispered to me, "We should ask Stan Roehrig to do that for us."

"Or we could just give our answers honestly," I said, and we both laughed. We didn't need to be coached to tell the truth. But as I thought about it, it struck me that it wasn't a half-bad idea, just in case we got nervous or tongue-tied on the stand. It might be nice to get a little direction in the heat of the moment. I jotted down a note about the signaling and passed it over to Stan. He read it and to my surprise, he jumped right up and asked for a recess and a word with the judge without the jury present.

Ibarra excused the jury and turned to Stan. "What's the problem, counselor?"

Stan explained what Lacy had been doing and only then did Tomono and I realize how wrong it was. Ibarra looked irate. He reprimanded Lacy, telling him that the court would not at all be tolerant of such behavior. Lacy looked guilty, like a kid who got caught cheating on a school test. He assured the court that it had been unintentional and that he'd make certain not to accidentally send any more signals to the witness. The jury came back in and the questioning continued.

Lacy stopped that day, but we noticed that the signaling was used from time to time throughout the trial. We never brought it to the attention of the judge again, however, and here's why: As it happens, there was a little snack shop in the courtroom operated by an older Japanese woman. Mrs. Sakamoto was a nice lady and I befriended her during the trial, sometimes bringing her roses from the farm, which she displayed on the counter. Every day, she would be in her shop selling sandwiches, candy bars, bags of chips, cigarettes, fruit, and other such items, typically watching soap operas on her small black and white TV when she wasn't serving customers. Mrs. Sakamoto was legally blind, but she could see enough to watch TV. The TV was up high, toward the back corner, and it faced the doorway to the shop, so Mrs. Sakamoto's back was typically to the door as she sat on her stool at the counter. There was a coffee machine just at the doorway and if all you wanted was coffee, you'd go to the machine, fill your cup, and walk to the counter to pay Mrs. Sakamoto the seventy-five cents that she charged.

One day, Mrs. Sakamoto confided in me that she didn't like some of the lawyers that came around. "Some of them fill their mugs with coffee and walk away without paying," she said.

"How do you know?" I asked, seeing as how the coffee machine was to her back as she watched her soaps.

"Because I can make out their reflections in my TV," she said. "They don't think I can see them, but I can."

I would learn that Mrs. Sakamoto knew a lot about the trial. Not only did the lawyers come into her shop, but during breaks, members of the jury did too. Of course, they weren't supposed to discuss the case with each other, but they often did. The first day of Lacy's signaling, Mrs. Sakamoto overheard one of the jurors talking about it to another. In turn, she mentioned it to me. "Those DuPont slimeballs are signaling to their witnesses," she told me. Now, the only time the signaling was discussed in the courtroom was after the jury had been excused. How did they know about it? It turns out that they had discovered it on their own. They saw what we saw. They saw Lacy nodding his head in different directions to elicit the answers he wanted.

I went back and reported my conversation with Mrs. Sakamoto to Stan and that's when we all agreed to say nothing more to the judge. "Let the jury see their attorneys cheating," said Stan. "The more they do it, the better for us!" From time to time, we continued to notice the signals. But now we knew that the jury noticed them, too.

Mrs. Sakamoto was astute. She'd sit on her stool watching her soaps, but always with one ear on the conversations of the jurors and lawyers coming in and out of her shop. They rarely noticed her, especially DuPont's lawyers. It wouldn't be like them, in their thousand-dollar suits, to pay any mind to a humble shop keeper. If they noticed at all, they just saw a little Japanese woman watching her old black and white television set. "They think I'm stupid," she would tell me. "They talk as if I'm not here. But just because I can't see well, that doesn't make me deaf." And, in fact, Mrs. Sakamoto didn't miss a thing. "You're having a good day today," she'd tell me whenever she picked up on some news that seemed to reflect favorably on our side. She would tell me bad news, too. "I think you're going to lose that motion your attorney filed this morning," she might say. There were days when she had more insight into the trial from her stool in the snack shop than I had from sitting in the courtroom.

Over time, Mrs. Sakamoto and I became good friends and several times she invited me to her home to have dinner with her and her husband. By then, I was spending most of the weeknights in Kona rather than traveling to and from Waimea every day. I knew nobody in Kona and some nights I got tired of hashing over the day's events of the trial with Stan and Andy and the others. Some nights I just wanted to get away from it all and it was a nice respite to spend an evening with the Sakamotos, enjoying a delicious, home-cooked Japanese meal. And in the courthouse, I kept making sure everyone on our side was paying for their coffees.

DuPont's attorneys, meanwhile, kept trying everything in the playbook, employing every trick of the trade. Two months into the trial, a sidebar, one of seemingly hundreds, took place up at Judge Ibarra's bench. With both side's lawyers hashing out some legal issue in low tones out of earshot of the jury box, the witness on the stand at the time, one of ours, turned to the jury and chuckled, "Don't they know it's not polite to whisper?" It was a small attempt at levity, but John Lacy heard it and saw another opportunity. "Your honor, their witness is talking to the jury!" he immediately declared. "We move for a mistrial!"

I didn't initially understand the seriousness of the matter, but Judge Ibarra excused the jury and then brought the members in one by one to interview them about what they'd heard. That's when I realized that two months of trial proceedings were at stake. We were all sweating it out as the interviews commenced. Most of the members said they'd heard the witness but what they heard was the innocuous remark about whispering. Some claimed not to have heard anything at all and, looking back, I wonder if these members had already been leaning toward our side. If so, Lacy's actions didn't help his case. The ploy may well have backfired. In the end, to our great relief, Judge Ibarra decided the comment had no bearing on the trial and the proceedings commenced. Out in the hallway, Stan let our witness know what he'd almost cost us in no uncertain terms.

One DuPont defense strategy, an ongoing one, was to delay or outright refuse to produce the documents we had repeatedly asked for in discovery. This had started well before the trial, of course, during the initial discovery period, notwithstanding the many sanctions levied against DuPont. But it continued far into the trial. One of the reasons was that there were other Benlate-related trials going on at the same time. New information was continually coming to light. In June of 1994, just as our trial was getting underway, a DuPont employee named Dennis Keeler was deposed for a Florida case and he testified to the existence of an eighty-four-page document DuPont had commissioned that summarized the results of Benlate testing. But in our case, DuPont hadn't turned this document over, even after an order to do so. Stan had to make a motion to compel, which Judge Ibarra granted, forcing DuPont to turn over the document.

Keeler testified in our trial, too. He took the stand in November. But after his testimony, we discovered that in another Florida deposition, Keeler had produced an additional four pages of test results that hadn't been included in the original eighty-four. DuPont was apparently hoping we weren't paying attention to any of the other cases that were underway. Again, we had to make a motion to compel and, again, Judge Ibarra ordered DuPont to comply. We subsequently entered those four pages into evidence, too.

DuPont also delayed in handing over the soil testing reports from Alta Analytical Laboratory, the lab that DuPont had used out of California. DuPont had claimed work–product privilege but the discovery master had reported to Judge Ibarra that we had shown a substantial need for the documents and our case would be unfairly prejudiced without them. Ibarra had ordered the documents turned over to us, but we still had to file a motion to compel. Finally, DuPont released two boxes of Alta documents.

Once my attorneys went through those boxes, it became obvious why DuPont had fought so hard to keep them from us. Steve Cox had the best understanding of the science and what he discovered in the documents was that Alta Analytical Laboratory had found DuPont-manufactured sulfonylureas in the soil of those four farms involved in the

Bush Ranch case, even though the Alta experts had testified during that trial in August of 1993 that *no* sulfonylureas had been found. We ultimately learned that Alta had found sulfonylureas in my soil, too, and in Tomono's, but just like in the Bush Ranch case, the Alta experts testified under oath that they had detected no sulfonylureas.

How did they get away with the false testimony? The two boxes of Alta documents showed that Liz Gilley of the Atlanta law firm of Alston and Bird, DuPont's legal representation for the Bush Ranch case, had instructed the Alta experts to raise their scientific detection limit after Gilley was advised that Alta had discovered sulfonylureas. Alta could actually detect sulfonylureas down to twenty-five parts per trillion, but when Alta faxed Gilley lab printouts that showed sulfonylureas had been detected in the Bush Ranch soils, she ordered them to change the detection threshold to fifty parts per trillion. This is what enabled Alta to generate reports and testify that sulfonylureas had not been found. In truth, they *had* been found, but not at the new threshold established at the behest of DuPont's Bush Ranch attorney. Or as Steve put it, "If you keep raising the blades of the lawnmower, sooner or later you're not going to cut any grass."

In point of fact, one of DuPont's own experts found that sulfonylureas damaged crops at the level of just *one* part per trillion. Our side found an expert who would testify that one-sixth of an ounce could kill the weeds of an entire acre of land. But DuPont's underlying data showing contamination at the lower level was never entered into evidence in the Bush Ranch trial, with DuPont claiming that anything under fifty parts per trillion was incapable of being detected or, at best, the detection would be unreliable. And just to cover all bases, Gilley further instructed Alta that if sulfonylureas were found at a higher level, to de-firm the results. In other words, she suggested outright falsification of the discoveries Alta had found. If there was a smoking gun to the case, this was it.

There was another one, too. In a file someone at DuPont had created, tellingly labeled "mucho problemo," we learned that the engine of a DuPont employee's car that had been parked outside of a DuPont facility showed the presence of a type of sulfonylurea that DuPont had claimed had never even been manufactured or sold in the United States. Little by little, DuPont's lies were being exposed.

By this time, with all of the discovery offenses, it seemed to me that Judge Ibarra was losing patience. Not only did he order DuPont to give us the Alta reports and allow them into evidence, we were allowed to question a witness, a Dr. Jodie Johnson, to interpret the reports for the jury, with DuPont prevented from cross-examining him. This was an especially damaging development for DuPont. Steve had Johnson on the stand and asked him if, from an analytical standpoint, he thought it was fraudulent for the witness in the Bush Ranch case to testify that there was no evidence of sulfonylureas in the Bush Ranch soil samples. "It would be fraudulent for anybody," Johnson answered.

And Judge Ibarra wasn't finished with DuPont. He promised to levy an additional punitive sanction at a later date. Indeed, before the trial would end, Ibarra would order DuPont to pay a sanction of $1.5 million to the State of Hawaii. Moreover, he would instruct the jury that DuPont had intentionally withheld evidence it had been ordered to produce, and advise the jury that they could consider that withholding in reaching their verdict. This was a big blow for DuPont, but it could have been worse. What Ibarra wouldn't tell them was that the attempt to keep the Alta documents from us had actually caused him to consider entering a default judgment against DuPont. A default judgment means *game over*. Judge Ibarra could have declared a victory for our side and the only thing the jury would have had to decide was how much money to award. Instead, Ibarra elected to let the trial play out.

As relentless as DuPont was in using whatever means possible to suppress evidence, we were not without our own little tricks to reveal it. To enter some of the more damaging documents into the trial itself, a little imagination was sometimes necessary. It wasn't as if you could just grab a document and start reading it to the jury. You needed a witness to present it on the stand. Our attorneys used what they called "the hotel lobby technique," the idea that all you need to do is just somehow get yourself into the metaphorical lobby. Stan or Steve would put someone on the stand who might have worked for one of the distributors. "Did you know about the dangers of Benlate?" they would ask. The witness would typically answer in the negative. Our attorney would continue: "So then DuPont didn't make you aware of this internal document that reveals a level of contamination?" They'd ask the witness to read from the document and now the document in question was in front of the jury. It didn't really matter who the witness was. The point was to find someone, anyone, to question as a means to introduce a damaging piece of evidence.

But DuPont was the master of suppression. In addition to work–product privilege, they argued of the logistical difficulties in obtaining information from the other lawsuits across the country. But Judge Ibarra knew about that central information depository DuPont had set up at their headquarters. He knew, in fact, that they had a full-time staff on duty there to coordinate all of the information being revealed in the many depositions and trials.

Judge Ibarra recognized that the pattern of withholding pertinent material extended well beyond his Kona courthouse. Plaintiffs everywhere were complaining about DuPont's willful refusal to release relevant documentation. We all came to realize that the decisions to withhold certain documents were not being made locally, but by DuPont at a corporate level. They were trying to maintain some kind of central control over the many trials and settlement negotiations going on around the country. It must have seemed to them like battling a large forest fire, with little brushfires popping up repeatedly here and there. You'd put one out, and another one would start someplace else. Or maybe it was more like an enormous game of whack-a-mole.

With the Alta results, it became clear why DuPont was so intent on keeping the documentation from being entered into its many court cases: Benlate had wreaked havoc on farms *everywhere*. And then came the revelation that there was even more evidence of cross contamination, not at the DuPont plant, but at Terra International, one of DuPont's packaging companies. In fact, this is where most of the contamination took place. One of our witnesses testified that the very machines that were used at the Terra plant to produce Benlate were also used to produce other pesticides and weedkillers. The production machines were huge, able to produce tons of Benlate at a time, and difficult to clean. The first run of Benlate through the machines would typically become contaminated with sulfonylureas. But rather than dump that run, which would have presented its own environmental problems, it would be set aside and added back into subsequent runs—a little here, a little there, just enough, presumably, to stay below DuPont's predetermined level of allowable contaminants.

The process was authorized by DuPont and DuPont countered in court that the Terra people used a colorimetric analysis to determine that the product was still safe. The analysis made use of a beam of light that was shown through the solution and read by receptors on the other side, determining the amount of sulfonylureas in the product and proving, to DuPont's satisfaction, that the amount was too low to make any difference. But the analysis was only done at certain intervals and batches of contaminated Benlate would often get missed. Worse, at one point, their colorimeter broke. Unable to repair it, they took to using a simple eye test until a new colorimeter was ordered. Instead of using a precision instrument, one of Terra's technicians would take a vial of the solution and hold it up to the light to see if the color looked right. Steve Cox had the technician on the stand. "And did you have your eyes properly calibrated?" he asked. This elicited some snickers from the jury and I sensed they were becoming more skeptical of DuPont with each passing day of the trial.

Above all else, with all of the testimony and evidence, we were showing that DuPont had known about the contamination for years. And it was this point that we tried to push home during the trial. Our attorneys asked not just for compensatory damages, but for punitive damages as well. It's one thing to cause damage. It's another to cause damage, know about it, and keep causing it.

SEVEN

Going for the Surfer Lawyer

As the trial proceeded, I noticed that the division of labor between my attorneys became more refined. Of Stan, Andy, and Steve, two of them were present in the courtroom each day. Then, getting a feel for how things were going that day, one of them would spend the next day preparing for the following day's witnesses. Stan was in court the majority of the time, with Andy and Steve doing most of the alternating.

Kris, in the meantime, spent his time doing research and writing legal briefs. Kris was the new kid. Originally from Michigan and with a law degree from Thomas M. Cooley Law School in his hometown of Lansing, he had come to the Big Island in 1988 to visit his brother, Guy, a tennis pro at

Mauna Lani. In 1990, with just three years of practicing law under his belt, he visited again and decided to stay, passing the Hawaii bar exam and taking a job with a small law firm in Hilo. In 1992, he got wind that Stan Roehrig and Andy Wilson, with the firm of Roehrig, Roehrig, Wilson, Hara, Schutte, and DeSilva were looking for an associate to help them with a big case against DuPont. He interviewed, got the job, and, shortly thereafter, I met him for the first time at my father's house when he stopped over to introduce himself as the new associate who would be working on our case. For the next year and a half, Kris cut his teeth on the discovery battles leading up to our trial.

Kris earned his paycheck. Practically every day during the trial, Judge Ibarra would ask for a memo from both sides about this or that legal issue. He always wanted to see the memos the next morning by eight o'clock and Kris would often end up working long into the night. There were nights, depending on the workload, where Kris wouldn't finish before morning, delivering briefs and research to Andy, Stan, and Steve over breakfast and only then falling into bed.

Strategy sessions in the condo were often fun to watch. My attorneys, even Stan and Andy with all their experience, were covering new ground and learning as they went. They'd handled big cases before, but nothing like this one. Surprisingly, for the entire duration of the trial, I never really saw them argue with each other. The discussions could be high-spirited, but it was mostly a lot of thinking out loud, albeit sometimes very loud. Listening to them hash out particular legal points gave me a sense of confidence in their knowledge and abilities.

Nevertheless, as the trial dragged on month after month, I began to feel the strain. There was the inherent stress of not knowing what the outcome was going to be, of course. Additionally, there was the financial stress. The expenses just kept piling up. The rented condos, the supplies, phone calls, photocopies, meals—it didn't seem like there was an end to it. And without being sure of the outcome, I had moments where I wondered if I was throwing good money after bad. Moreover, I couldn't spend any time on the farm, which was, of course, my livelihood, the only place where the money to pay all those expenses was coming from. Fortunately, I'd left competent people in charge and the business was able to continue fairly seamlessly. Things were not going quite so smoothly with my marriage, however. Not only was I absent from the farm, I was absent from home. Joanne had come to the courtroom for the opening arguments and for the first few days of testimony, but how can you ask anyone to sit through day after day of trial for seven months? Joanne had her own business, a floral business at a resort, and she needed to be there. The separation was putting a strain on our marriage. Just one more cost that I was discovering.

Of course, I wasn't the only one bearing the costs. My attorneys were all in. To me, they seemed assured and I don't ever remember them even once indicating that we might ultimately end up losing. Maybe they didn't want to appear negative in front of me. Or maybe they really believed in the case. Nevertheless, it had to have kept them up at nights. The case became so time-consuming that Stan and Andy had long since stopped taking on new clients. Tomono and I were it. Yes, we helped defray some of their day-to-day costs, but Stan and Andy had no income and they still had overhead—their Hilo offices and the salaries of Kris and the secretaries, not to mention their own personal expenses. The firm had a significant line of credit with the bank based on years of success, but before the trial would end, that line of credit would be completely exhausted. The bank increased it a couple of times, but, eventually, both Stan and Andy would have to take out second mortgages on their homes. Andy would go a step further and take out a mortgage on his mother's condo as well as a little vacation home he and his wife owned in Kapoho, about forty-five minutes from Hilo. Stan and Andy couldn't afford to stay in and they couldn't afford to get out. Essentially, they had pushed all their chips into the middle of the table. They were going to win the case, or they were going to lose everything.

For Steve's part, he put $100,000 of his own money into the case, and for the duration of the trial—a trial we all expected would last weeks, not months—he moved to the Big Island, away from his wife in San Francisco. She came out to visit once, staying for three weeks and making a vacation of it. Turns out she was a good cook. One day, she decided to cook everyone dinner and while court was in session, she walked down the road and came across a street vendor who had a twenty-pound tuna for sale. She took it back to the condo, only to discover the only two knives in the place were as dull as the spoons. She hacked away at the tuna, trying desperately to filet it. Steve helped when he got back to the condo, and by the time those two had finished preparing the tuna, it looked like it had been beaten up by a heavyweight boxer. But as bad as it looked, it tasted delicious.

Kris, though he didn't have the same financial stake in the case, felt the pressure, too. It wasn't just the hard work he put in so many days and nights, but the fact that his entire career was now focused solely on our case. Like the other attorneys, whole years of his life would be devoted to it. I wondered if, when he took the position at Roehrig Wilson, he could have imagined what he was getting himself into. But for Kris, there was a silver lining at least. Maybe it was the shared stress and the closeness of working together, but as it happened, he and Stan's secretary, Jeri, had begun a romance shortly after Kris had started working at the firm.

The romance was kept secret for months. Kris was hesitant to tell Stan who was rather possessive with his secretarial staff. In fact, there was a sign outside of Stan's outer office door that read: "Roehrig's Girls." Plus, the firm was now fully engaged with the case. Kris worried about the perceived impropriety of his relationship with a secretary of the firm at such a critical time. On the other hand, he knew he couldn't keep the relationship secret forever. On the long flight back to Hawaii from that Orlando meeting of Benlate plaintiff attorneys, Kris, sitting next to Stan the whole way, finally mustered up the nerve to tell him about the romance. Maybe it was the positive energy they were riding from the meeting. Maybe it was the relative safety of breaking the news in a crowded plane at 35,000 feet where Stan was less likely to react in an angry outburst. Or maybe it was the in-flight cocktails. Whatever the reason, Kris broke the news. Stan reacted with silence. Cold silence that continued for the duration of the flight—six-and-a-half hours, to this day a flight that Kris considers to be the most awkward and uncomfortable of his life. The next morning, it was business as usual in the office and nothing was said about the disclosure from the day before. Stan apparently accepted the circumstances, an acceptance that might have been easier had he understood that this was no mere trivial fling. Ultimately, Kris and Jeri would marry and have two children. They're still together today, living happily in Hilo.

Like everyone else involved in the case, the secretaries worked hard, too. It was a true team effort. Stan had two secretaries, including Kris's future wife, and Andy also had two. Because of the two-hour drive between Hilo and Kona, the secretaries agreed to alternate. One week, one of Andy's secretaries and one of Stan's secretaries would stay the week in Kona, living out of one of the condos Tomono and I rented for the firm. The next week, the other two secretaries would spend the week. It could not have been easy, and the secretaries—Jeri Shiroma, Chris Kamaka, Mary Jo Chong, and Kanoe Lum Ho—all made great personal sacrifices in the course of the trial.

The close quarters of the staff condo presented its own share of challenges. First, the boxes and boxes of documents created a maze the occupants had to navigate.

Each morning, shirts and pants needed to be ironed and it was often hectic for everybody to get around and dressed without getting in each other's way. A secretary burst in on one of the attorneys one morning who was just starting to dress and wearing nothing more than his boxers. In the evening, meals were often noisily prepared and eaten while somebody, typically Kris, was begging for peace and quiet to prepare the next morning's brief. Nerves began to fray. Despite these conditions, everyone did their best to be team players and accept the circumstances, coming together to produce the kind of concerted effort needed to withstand the rigors of a trial against the likes of DuPont.

What helped the staff was to unwind at the end of the day. Happy hour, or *pau hana*, became a daily ritual for keeping everyone's sanity. Most evenings would involve a drink or two on the lanai of the condo, but on particularly stressful days, Stan and Andy's staff needed to go out, *sans* Stan and Andy. On those days, Steve Cox was a godsend, always willing to take the staff out for dinner at his expense. Sometimes, it was an ocean-side table at a fine Kona dining establishment like Jameson's By The Sea or Huggo's; sometimes it was fish tacos or burgers up the mountainside at Drysdale's Pub. And Steve knew his wines. He'd always order the most expensive on the list, quenching many a thirst and restoring morale. Everyone would retire to the condos rejuvenated and ready to face another day of trial.

But the pressure never stayed away for long. Each day brought about its own unique challenges, and in the back of everyone's mind was the idea that nobody really knew how things were ultimately going to play out. There was, however, one particular point in the trial when we all started feeling pretty good about it. One of the witnesses, a professor there on DuPont's behalf, was a Southern gentleman who always wore a white suit and spoke in a kindly drawl. Stan took to calling him Mint Julep Man. As it turned out, Mint Julep Man once worked for Crawford and Company, a large insurance claims management group and the company DuPont used to help settle their early Benlate claims.

In his role with Crawford, Mint Julep Man had visited several damaged farms, finding that Benlate had been the reason for the crop damage, and settling with the farmers in lieu of any further legal action. It's important to note that back when the contamination was first being discovered, DuPont was happy to acknowledge it. They were insured. Damages were paid out by their insurer and DuPont wasn't coming out of pocket. Only when their insurance had been exhausted did they change their tune and, therefore, their tactics. Suddenly, their Benlate was safe. And now, Mint Julep Man was on the stand testifying to its presumably safe qualities.

Stan and Andy only found out about Mint Julep Man's role with Crawford on the evening before their cross-examination. Word had gotten to them from one of the other plaintiff's attorneys on the mainland. In fact, one of Mint Julep Man's reports blaming Benlate for the crop damage on one particular farm was in one of the boxes of evidence back at Stan and Andy's office in Hilo. They called one of their secretaries that night who dug for hours through the boxes, found the report, and drove over to Kona with it at two o'clock in the morning. When the courtroom opened, Stan and Andy presented the document to Judge Ibarra for admission. Naturally, DuPont argued that it was too late. Ibarra took his time reading the document and said, "I'm admitting the evidence. Otherwise it would be a miscarriage of justice."

How that evidence was admitted turned out to be high drama, the kind of scene you might see in an old Perry Mason episode. That morning in the courtroom, with Mint Julep Man on the stand, Stan had him repeat his testimony from the day before that Benlate was safe. Then he placed the Crawford document on an overhead projector, flashing it on a screen for the jury to see.

"Sir, is this a report about Benlate?" Stan asked the witness, pointing to the screen.

"Yes sir, it appears to be so," said Mint Julep Man in his Southern drawl.

"And would you mind reading what it says there?"

Mint Julep Man read the words, the words that said that Benlate had caused the damage done to the crops of the farmer in question.

"And could you tell the court, please, who signed this document?" Stan pressed.

Mint Julep Man had no choice but to admit, sheepishly, that the affixed signature was none other than his own. Notwithstanding his prior testimony that Benlate was safe, he had earlier signed a document for DuPont's claims management company that Benlate was responsible for crop damage. At this, we all noticed the reaction of the jury, in particular, the reaction of a middle-aged Filipino woman sitting in the front of the jury box. She turned her head and exhaled with an unambiguous grunt of disgust.

That. That was the point where I think we all started feeling better about our chances.

Meanwhile, our trial was getting lots of media attention from around the country as other farmers watched eagerly to see what the outcome was going to be. All the major papers ran stories about the case, including the *Wall Street Journal.* Kris had been designated the media spokesman and handled requests for interviews and information. A trial in a little courtroom in a Hawaiian town most people had never heard of was suddenly big news. In the end, however, it wouldn't be the biggest trial of its time. Not by a long shot. Just as our case was winding down, a much, much bigger case was taking place in a Los Angeles courtroom: *People of the State of California v. Orenthal James Simpson.* It's hard for me not to draw parallels. Both defendants had dream teams of legal representation. Both defendants had money to burn.

The funny thing is, around this time I ordered a new vehicle. It obviously wasn't the best time to be spending money, but my old car was routinely breaking down and I needed something more reliable. I ordered a Ford Bronco, unaware, until it arrived on the island, that it was the exact same model and color as the Bronco OJ Simpson made famous with the car chase seen on TV nationwide. "Looks like you got the OJ Simpson special," the dealer smiled when I went to pick up the car. Suddenly, I no longer wanted it.

But the dealer wouldn't take it back and I was stuck. Worse, I found that it drove poorly around the island. In time, I would replace it, but the trade-in value was such that it wasn't worth trading in. I couldn't find anybody to buy it, either. To this day, I have that Ford Bronco, a reminder of those strange days.

Finally, our trial neared its end. The parade of witnesses came and went. We rested, the defense rested, and both sides prepared to give their closing arguments. But even then, DuPont was still looking for a way to slither out of trouble. Yet one more time they tried for a mistrial. This came on the heels of a *Wall Street Journal* article that disclosed the $1.5 million sanction against DuPont. John Lacy demanded everybody meet in Judge Ibarra's chamber one morning where he threw a copy of the *Journal* onto his desk, complaining about the ostensible leak. "Our case is being tried in the press!" he huffed. Kris LaGuire would speak later about the sudden sinking feeling in the pit of his stomach at that moment. It was he who had clued the *Wall Street Journal* in on the sanction. What kind of trouble had he just gotten our side into?

Judge Ibarra read the article and said, "Counselor, I didn't issue any gag orders on this trial. There's nothing improper here. Is there anything else?" Lacy had to admit that there was not, and Kris was able to breathe again.

And so, the closing arguments commenced. Stan Roehrig's was riveting. He summarized the testimony of key witnesses and relevant documents. He talked about Alta Laboratory and Mint Julep Man and Dennis Keeler's testimony about the eighty-four-page document summarizing the contaminated lots of Benlate. He talked about the devastation of my farm and Tomono's farm, and how DuPont, a $38 billion company, needed to be held accountable and, indeed, punished for their egregious actions in providing the contaminated product and trying to cover it up by withholding important documentation from us. It was a stirring argument and I watched as a few of the jurors nodded along. Lacy's closing argument was more subdued, with him touting the virtues of DuPont's science and claiming there hadn't been sufficient proof given that Tomono or I had sustained any significant damage. Stan then had the final opportunity to speak to the jury and he effectively poked holes in Lacy's closing argument.

After that, Judge Ibarra turned the case over to the jury, giving them a lengthy list of instructions. There were several matters they needed to rule on, including, first of all, whether DuPont's Benlate was responsible for the damage to our farms. Then, if they found DuPont responsible, they had to decide the amount of damages and how to apportion them between Tomono's farm and mine. Additionally, besides economic damages, were restoration damages appropriate? Did we deserve to be recompensed for soil restoration and replacement of farm structures? Finally, the jury had to decide if punitive damages were warranted. On the matter of product liability, a simple preponderance of the evidence was sufficient. For the matter of punitive damages, the jury had to believe that DuPont "clearly and convincingly" acted recklessly or reprehensibly, and with intent. And, of course, as he said he would, Ibarra instructed the jury that DuPont had intentionally withheld evidence that it had been ordered to produce, advising the members of the jury that they could consider that withholding in reaching their verdict. At long last, the jury was sent to their chambers and we all retired to the condos to wait.

Meanwhile, DuPont was still doing everything they could to minimize their potential damages and keep from facing responsibility. Prior to the closing arguments they had flown in their top in-house attorney, Jerry Ashby, a heavyset guy with an ever-present cigar in his mouth. Ashby reported directly to DuPont's board of directors. Now, with the jury in deliberation, he approached our attorneys with a settlement offer of $3 million. "You've put a lot of time and effort into this, haven't you?" he said, chomping on his cigar. "I know you've got bills to pay. Mortgages and so forth. You haven't had any income in quite some time. Are you willing to take a risk on the jury? Juries can be surprising, you know. Three million is nice insurance when you stop and think about it. What do you say?"

It didn't work. The offer was an insult. He upped it to $5 million, which was still an insult. Stan told him so and he left for the airport. Frankly, by then, we knew we were going to win the case. The evidence was too strong and DuPont's attempts to cover up their culpability were too obvious to ignore. The question was not whether we would win, but by how much.

The jury deliberated for the rest of the day. And all of the following day. Finally, on the afternoon of the third day,

January 26, 1995, two days after opening arguments began in the OJ Simpson case, the jury came back into our courtroom with their verdict. Word got out to everyone and we all rushed for the courthouse with the attorneys throwing their jackets and ties on as we swept into the courtroom.

"Ladies and gentlemen of the jury," Judge Ibarra began, "have you reached a verdict?"

"We have, Your Honor," reported the jury foreman. Then he handed the jury forms—all the questions the jury had been tasked with resolving—to the bailiff who turned them over to Judge Ibarra. Ibarra began reading them to himself, taking his time to make sure he understood what the jury had decided. It probably took him five minutes, but it seemed like thirty. Hardly anyone breathed.

Finally, Judge Ibarra turned to the foreman and asked him what the jury's verdict was on all of the issues. The foreman responded that the jury had found there was a defect in the manufacture or design of the Benlate sold to us, DuPont was negligent with their product, and their negligence caused damage to our crops. Further, they found that not only was DuPont liable for the damage, but by clear and convincing evidence, they were also liable for punitive damages. Then came the monetary amounts they had settled on: $9.5 million in compensatory damages and $14.3 million in punitive damages—$23.8 million total.

What they didn't give us were damages for the soil restoration and for farm structural damage. The evidence was not sufficiently convincing to them that long-term damage was sustained that would require the replacement of the soil or the buildings. This disappointed us. But $23.8 million was nothing to sneeze at. The bottom line was that after all those months, we had won. We were victorious. We had defeated Goliath.

But John Lacy had one more move left that day and he used it. He asked Judge Ibarra to poll the jury. This means asking each juror how he or she decided. In a civil trial, a unanimous verdict is not required. All we needed was nine jurors out of the twelve to decide for us on each issue. Lacy's hope was that if there were two or three who decided against us, that would give him some grounds for appeal. But it turned out that *nobody* had decided against us on any of the issues. The jury's decisions had been unanimous on all points.

Judge Ibarra then dismissed the jury, thanking them for their service. On their way out, everyone on our side thanked the jury, too, but how do you sufficiently express gratitude for the sacrifices these people made, putting their lives on hold for seven months, with nothing at stake for them except wanting to do the right thing? When factoring in the true costs of a trial, I don't imagine anyone ever stops to consider the time the jury members have to surrender.

In contemplating their decision, what swayed them to our side was surely a preponderance of things. We'd certainly presented enough evidence. The way that Lacy had been signaling to his witnesses was most likely a factor. Maybe it was DuPont's blatant hiding of documentation, including those damning Alta Laboratory results. Dr. Jodie Johnson's characterization of the Bush Ranch testimony as "fraudulent" sure didn't help their side. Ibarra's instruction to the jury that DuPont had withheld evidence was a brutal blow to their case. Of course, one final straw had to have been the testimony of Mint Julep Man. A couple of years later, we would learn that something else might have helped sway the jury. One of the jury members confessed that they'd never forgotten what one of the members of the original jury pool had said about Stan Roehrig: "I see him when the waves are big," he'd said. This juror summed up the decision process like so: "We decided to go for the surfer lawyer."

However it was decided, I felt relieved it was all over. In fact, I felt much more relief than joy. After all this time, I could get now back to my farm and get on with my life. The only problem was, we had to collect. And I would learn that winning a court award and collecting it are two entirely different things. I thought the end of the trial meant we had crossed the finish line. But I soon discovered that we still had a long, long way to go.

EIGHT
Appeal

In May of 1995, Judge Ibarra entered judgments for our side totaling roughly $25.2 million, increasing the amount the jury had awarded us. He added approximately $750,000 for court costs, $291,000 for costs associated with DuPont's discovery abuse, and $286,000 in interest. Of course DuPont also owed the State of Hawaii $1.5 million for the punitive sanction.

In August, DuPont appealed. This was hardly a surprise, even with the unanimous verdicts on every issue. DuPont was still using its battle of attrition strategy, dragging things out, hoping Stanley Tomono and I would run out of money and simply drop out. Their basis for appeal rested on several technicalities, but a major point of contention was Judge Ibarra's talk to the jury about DuPont's discovery misconduct. It didn't seem to matter that everything he told them about DuPont's refusal to comply with the proper discovery process was true. DuPont argued that the explanation to the jury was prejudicial and unfair.

Stan and Andy brought in a Honolulu attorney by the name of Peter Esser who specialized in appeals. Unbeknownst to me at the time, the appeal process is its own unique area of the law, requiring someone with a different skillset and body of legal knowledge. My expenses, in other words, kept adding up, even after the verdict in our favor. Meanwhile, DuPont hired their own attorneys for the appeal—Crowell & Moring out of Washington, DC, who dispatched a representative named Patrick Lee.

The appeal process ran directly from Judge Ibarra's courtroom in Kona to the Supreme Court of the State of Hawaii in Honolulu. Naturally, like everything else associated with our legal action against DuPont, it was going to take months to get there. In the interim, the Supreme Court had an appellate mediation program that required the parties to engage in mediation as a means by which to settle the case. Presumably, DuPont would offer us something less than what the jury had awarded us and in return for our acceptance, they'd drop the appeal.

The mediation took place in October in Honolulu, in the Hawaii Supreme Court building in front of Edward King, an attorney of counsel with a Honolulu law firm. King was also a judge and mediator. Stan Roehrig, Stanley Tomono and his wife Cynthia, and Joanne and I were all there. Patrick Lee was there with some other DuPont attorneys. Immediately upon our arrival, King had some disconcerting news for us. He had just joined the firm of Goodsill, Anderson, Quinn, and Stifel—DuPont's Hawaii law firm, the firm of John Lacy. He made the disclosure assuring us he could be impartial but wanting to give us the opportunity to request another mediator. This would mean rescheduling. No one on our side was happy with this news, but after discussing it, we opted to proceed nonetheless. We were already there, after all, and we decided to take Judge King at his word that he would be fair to us.

Their side met with Judge King first, taking about an hour to present their side of the case and their settlement offer. Then we met with King, who let us know what DuPont was willing to do, namely, offer us $7 million to go away. This was only slightly higher than the amount we'd been offered by Jerry Ashby while the jury had been in deliberations. We were speechless. DuPont wanted to cut the award down by more than 72 percent.

Roehrig rose and began arguing the facts of the case to Judge King, but I'd already heard enough. I happened to be sitting next to Cynthia and I leaned over to her and whispered, "I'm walking out. Why don't you follow me?" Cynthia nodded. I got up and interrupted Stan's argument by whispering in his ear what we were doing. Cynthia rose and we started out. Joanne followed, and then Stanley Tomono fell in right behind. Roehrig stopped his argument to inform Judge King of what was certainly obvious to him by then: the deal was unacceptable. Judge King nodded. I think he understood.

We strode out of the courthouse in view of the other side's attorneys. "Wait, where are you going?" asked Lee.

"We're way too far apart," Stan replied. "We don't see any reason to stick around for anymore."

"But…but we're negotiating."

"I'm sorry," said Stan, "but I think we're done negotiating."

Lee faxed a letter to Judge King the next day outlining DuPont's rationale for the low number and King, in turn, faxed it to Stan and Andy. It was "with disbelief," wrote Lee, that we rejected the offer. "The plaintiffs either do not understand or did not consider the vulnerability of their position on appeal," adding that, "the entire verdict, and especially the punitive damages, are vulnerable because of Judge Ibarra's unprecedented jury instruction regarding withholding of documents."

Tellingly, Lee wrote this as partial justification for the offered amount: "Our offer of $7 million is four times larger than the annual gross revenue of the Kawamata and Tomono operations. Our offer was clearly a windfall to these two growers." So that was it; they weren't interested in fair and just compensation. They'd simply arrived at a number that they had calculated would be a "windfall" for us. In their minds, it was enough money to buy us off; $7 million should have been sufficient to make us go away.

Stan faxed a letter back to Judge King the following day. "Contrary to DuPont's representations that the likelihood of reversal is great, DuPont's chances of success are extremely remote. We are fully prepared to see this appeal through to the end if that is what it will take to force DuPont to pay its just debts to our clients." He closed with, "Please formally close these mediation proceedings. *Mahalo*."

The year closed out with no more settlement offers forthcoming and there was nothing left to do but wait for the appeal to find its way before the state Supreme Court. Stan Roehrig got some good news as 1996 began: because of our trial, he was named the Hawaii Bar Association's Lawyer of the Year for 1995. Needless to say, I thought it was well earned. Other than that bright spot, however, these were nerve-wracking days. We'd come so far. We'd won in the trial court, but I knew that verdicts could be reversed. That's why appeals courts exist, after all.

In March 1996, DuPont filed their opening brief with the Supreme Court. We responded with our answering brief in June. This, I discovered, was no easy mission. A big part of the problem is that you have to summarize your position and the facts that support that position in a very limited space. Normally, the court allows thirty pages. Because of the length of our trial, we were granted sixty, but it was still hardly enough. There were seven months of trial transcripts and thousands of exhibits, not to mention the two-plus years of discovery disputes that were a big part of the appeal as well. And it wasn't enough to refute a point factually; you had to refute it legally. If you refer to a statement or document, you have to show where in the trial court record it was admitted. In the days of paper transcripts, you couldn't simply do a digital search. Moreover, there was a preponderance of case law that was referred to. DuPont cited other legal cases, forcing my attorneys to research those cases and cite cases for our side. It was a painstaking, three-month process that my attorneys confessed ended up requiring a level of legal research and writing that none of them had ever been involved in. Peter Esser flew into Hilo several times. So did Steve Cox. All of the attorneys worked hard to convey our arguments and condense all of the relevant issues into a cogent document for the appeals court to consider.

Then, DuPont had their chance to file a reply brief. These were all preliminaries before the Supreme Court would ultimately hear oral argument before deciding the appeal. Because of the court backlog, our case would not be decided until December 1997, almost *three years* after the jury's verdict.

While we waited, a huge break came our way. During the trial, Steve Cox had sent those Alta Analytical Laboratory reports, the ones that showed soil contamination, to the Bush Ranch plaintiffs' attorneys in Atlanta. Alta's experts had testified in that trial that sulfonylureas had not been found in the plaintiffs' soil, but as might be recalled, somewhere in those boxes of lab reports that DuPont finally handed over to us, we had discovered evidence that DuPont's attorney in that case, Liz Gilley, had instructed the experts to raise the threshold of the detection limit. More egregiously, she'd actually directed them to de-firm—falsify—the results. Bush Ranch and the other three plaintiffs in that suit had settled for a mere $4 million. This was the case that DuPont's chairman Edgar S. Woolard Jr. had called a victory. No wonder. Had the Bush Ranch plaintiffs received the Alta information during their trial, they could have been awarded tens—perhaps hundreds—of millions of dollars.

Armed with this new information, the Bush Ranch plaintiffs went back to court where US District Judge Robert Elliott fined DuPont a whopping $101 million, calling DuPont's hiding of those Alta documents "willful, deliberate, conscious, purposeful, deceitful, and in bad faith," furthermore saying that the concealment of the documents "affected the rulings and the orders of the court and interfered with the administration of justice." The discovery abuse "rendered the trial a farce."[5] He could have added that the settlement had a direct bearing on the subsequent settling of those 220 cases in April 1994. Remember, it was the settlement of the Bush Ranch case that induced the other growers to settle. DuPont appealed the $101 million sanction, of course, with Chairman Woolard calling it an "unreasonable decision."[6]

In the end, the sanction was significantly reduced. Nevertheless, of interest to us was that, in the course of the hearing in front of Judge Elliott, Liz Gilley was summoned before the judge and admitted that by entering the Alta documents into the Bush Ranch case (albeit with falsified results), DuPont had waived their work-product privilege, the very thing that they had claimed in our case as far back as discovery. In other words, when we had originally asked for those documents, DuPont knew they were no longer protected. And yet they lied about the status of them.

Based upon Gilley's admission that their work-product claim had been a complete misrepresentation, my attorneys prepared a Rule 60(b) motion which seeks the admission of evidence *after* a trial has concluded, based upon fraud or other major misconduct. It's the trial court's job to address such a motion, but because the case was already on appeal, we had to first present a copy of the Rule 60(b) motion to the Supreme Court, requesting permission to file it before Judge Ibarra. In our case, specifically, the motion was to send the matter back to Judge Ibarra for him to hold another sanction hearing against DuPont. Filing the motion was more strategic than punitive. By filing the motion with the Supreme Court—the same body that was scheduled to hear the appeal—the Supreme Court was put on notice as to DuPont's deceit, which could only help us when the appeal would ultimately get underway. Such a motion isn't always successful. More times than not, it goes nowhere. In our case, the Supreme Court granted the motion and there was yet one more hearing in front of Ibarra and one more sanction placed against DuPont, perhaps the most important sanction of all.

At the additional sanction hearing, Judge Ibarra was less than amused by DuPont's concealment of the Alta documents with their deceitful claim of work-product privilege. "DuPont," Ibarra ruled, "engaged in fraud and intentional misconduct," and "acted in bad faith, wantonly and for oppressive reasons." In addition to upholding his previous $1.5 million sanction, he assessed DuPont additional attorneys' fees for all the work my attorneys had to perform with respect to the false claim of work-product. Moreover, Ibarra stated that had he known of DuPont's misrepresentation of the work-product claim prior to holding our trial, he would have entered a default judgment against DuPont. Most importantly for us, all of this played out before the appeal was even heard. As a result, the Supreme Court got a taste of what we'd been dealing with all along. The Rule 60(b) motion and Judge Ibarra's ruling did a lot of our arguing for us. Stan called it *maunu*, the Hawaiian word for bait or chum. "If you're going after the big fish, you need all the *maunu* you can get," he said.

In the meantime, we had a potentially damaging development taking place on our side of the case. Stanley and Cynthia began talking about getting a divorce. As with Joanne and me, the Tomonos had been feeling the stresses and strains of the lawsuit. There seemed to be no end in sight to the legal proceedings, which were all-consuming. As with most divorces, there was some acrimony and a goodly amount of disagreement over the assets. In fact, they'd both hired divorce lawyers. Stan Roehrig cautioned the Tomonos. "We can't allow DuPont to get wind of this," he told them. "If they know you're squabbling over money and property, that will leave us in a vulnerable position." Roehrig was still hoping for a settlement that we could all live with. "Your divorce proceedings could weaken our ability to negotiate," he said. "We need to show strength and unity. We need to get this resolved."

The Tomonos needed to settle their differences quickly. What they needed was a mediator of their own, someone fair and impartial who could recommend how their assets should be rightfully split up. Their choice floored me. They both agreed that the mediator should be me. "We trust you," said Cynthia. "We know you'll be fair." I tried to argue that I knew nothing about mediating divorces, but they both felt that anything would be better than continuing to pay their divorce lawyers who had essentially done nothing up to that point except bill the Tomonos around $40,000 each. It had become clear that the lawyers knew about the pending DuPont settlement and were purposely dragging things out, hoping to get a small piece of the settlement pie.

Then Andy and Stan both appealed to me. "For the good of our case against DuPont," is how Andy put it. I finally agreed and the Tomonos came to see me in my office where I taped a big sheet of blank paper to the wall. I drew a line down the middle and wrote "Stanley" at the top of one side and "Cynthia" at the top of the other. Then I asked them to start listing their assets. Stanley would say he wanted this and Cynthia would say she wanted that. I placed the various items in their respective columns unless there was a disagreement on an item, in which case I wrote that item down on a separate sheet of paper. When we got through with all the assets, we started talking about the items on the "disagreement" sheet. On each one, I'd ask both parties what the item was worth to them. "Stanley," I'd say, "how about if you compensate Cynthia for that with $10,000?" Or, "Cynthia, how about you trade item seven for item twelve?"

We met twice, each time for several hours. The process worked. Both sides finally agreed to everything and I wrote up a settlement agreement that they signed. We sent the agreement to their respective attorneys who wrote it up in all the proper legalese and filed it with the court. And that was that. I did something the high-priced divorce lawyer couldn't—or more likely, wouldn't—do. I managed to walk the Tomonos through a divorce where both sides came away feeling as though they'd been treated fairly.

Finally, in early 1997, the appeal came before the Hawaii Supreme Court in Honolulu for oral argument: five robed justices sitting in high, leather-backed chairs behind a long bench of beautiful Hawaiian koa wood, several feet above the tables where the parties and attorneys sat. I wouldn't have to say anything and yet still felt intimidated by the aura of the room. Our attorneys were there and DuPont's attorneys were there, including Patrick Lee from Washington. Before the justices appeared, both sets of attorneys hashed out the finer points of the proceedings. Andy Wilson became the unofficial spokesperson for our side and a young female attorney was the unofficial spokesperson for theirs, both of them meeting in between the counsel tables. Apparently, I wasn't the only one intimidated by the venue. Every time Andy would suggest some procedural point, the young female attorney would respond, "Hang on, let me check." Then she'd go back to the defendant's side of the room to confer and come back with an answer.

Finally, after most everything had been agreed to with the young woman running back and forth, Andy asked her, "Well, do you want to go first, or should we?"

"Hang on," she said, "let me check." After a few moments conferring with the DuPont guys, she returned and said, "We think the most fair thing would be to flip a coin."

"Sure," said Andy, taking a quarter out of his pocket. "Heads or tails?"

The young woman thought for a second and then replied, "Hang on, let me check."

At any rate, the proceedings finally got underway. DuPont restated their arguments, harping especially on the jury instruction Judge Ibarra had given. Additionally, they argued for the limitation of liability provision that was part of the Benlate product label, asserting that Ibarra had been wrong to rule against the disclaimer. "It's very narrow," argued Patrick Lee with respect to the limitation, "but it runs very deep." It sounded eloquent, but in essence, their case boiled down to forgetting about all that had happened at the trial, including the discovery issues. They had a tough climb to make and they couldn't make it. In the end, the Supreme Court upheld the verdict. I couldn't help but think the repeated concealment of documents had a lot to do with their decision, especially since the court had granted the Rule 60(b) motion and they knew that Judge Ibarra had ruled, in the interim, that DuPont had engaged "in fraud and intentional misconduct."

My attorneys mentioned to me something else that helped ensure the sustaining of the verdict: the damage amounts had been reasonable. Sometimes, a jury can go overboard and if it awards a ridiculous sum of money, an appeal might be more likely to succeed. We concluded that a good portion of the jury's two-and-a-half day deliberation in our trial was probably spent with the jury carefully arriving at their final numbers. Their circumspection was just one more reason to be grateful for their hard work.

But even after the Hawaii Supreme Court ruling, it still wasn't over. DuPont had one more court they could appeal to: the United States Supreme Court. It was yet another way of dragging things out further and it seemed clear that DuPont was going to use it.

DuPont had until April 13, 1998 to file their appeal, and we could do nothing but wait. From time to time, Andy or Stan would ask us if we wanted to reconsider a settlement. "How much would you be willing to settle for at this point?" they'd say. For my part, I'd become completely disgusted with the whole process and one day, after being asked one more time about a possible settlement amount, I said, "Nothing less than what Judge Ibarra awarded us, plus interest. I'll walk away with nothing before I agree to compromise with DuPont." And then I made it final. "Please don't ever ask me again, guys." And they never did.

By then, with interest, the amount of the award had grown substantially. But I had given up on the idea of ever seeing a penny of it. In my mind, I walked away from the whole ordeal, telling myself that if I ever collected anything, that would be fine. If not, which seemed much more likely, I'd sell the farm since I would no longer be able to afford to keep it running, and find another way to make a living. I'd spent far too much time on DuPont as it was. I decided even another minute wasn't worth it.

In late March, to get away from everything, I took a much-needed vacation—a fishing trip to Mexico with

Joanne, our daughter, Leilyn, and Joanne's mother, where we stayed in an old Baja Mexican village hotel. We came in from fishing one day and the old man that worked the check-in desk told me that I'd missed a phone call from Stan Roehrig. I picked up the phone at the desk to call him back and the old man said, "Make sure you speak quickly, *señor*. The connection can go dead at any time here. Plus, *por favor*, it's five American dollars per minute."

I got a hold of Stan, who said, "Raymond, we settled the case."

"Stan," I said, "how could you do that? I told you I didn't want anything less than the full amount! I'm not going to settle."

"Raymond, listen," Stan replied, "you don't understand. We *got* the full amount. Including interest. They've conceded defeat. They're not going to take the case to the US Supreme Court. Apparently, DuPont has a new CEO. He's taken a look at how much all of this has cost the company. He wants to cut their losses. It's over. We won. The money is already in a bank account ready for disbursement. I have Stanley Tomono's signature. All we need is yours. Come see me as soon as you get home."

I hung up the phone and handed ten bucks to the old man, barely able to believe what I'd just heard. The next day we moved on to La Paz where Leilyn caught a fish so big that, had we entered it, she would have won the tournament that happened to be going on at the time. But catching the fish was enough for us. We'd won something bigger back in Hawaii. I let the victory sink in as I enjoyed the warm

Mexican sun. When we returned to the Big Island, I rushed over to Stan's house from the airport and signed the document. It was three years after the verdict, six years after the start of the case, and almost a decade after my employee came up to me with those discolored bridal pink roses. Justice had finally been served. But the cost had been steep.

NINE

DuPont: Business as Usual

On a warm Miami day in 1989, Donna Castillo, two months' pregnant, went for her daily walk, pushing her daughter in a stroller. They passed by a strawberry and tomato farm and Donna could see that a tractor had become stuck in the mud of the field. The tractor had a spraying mechanism, which was apparently still open, and as the driver jerked the tractor back and forth to try to free it from the muck, a large plume of mist was released into the air, dousing Donna with a liquid that was odorless and colorless. "Probably just water," her husband later assured her.

But seven months later, to her and her husband's horror, Donna gave birth to a boy with a severe birth defect, a rare condition called anophthalmia. Their son Johnny was born with no eyes.

Donna eventually joined an international anophthalmia parents' support group, and in the process, learned something interesting. As it turns out, there was a cluster of anophthalmia birth defect cases in the farming town of Fife, Scotland. And there was a common thread. It was suspected that the mothers of the babies born with no eyes had all been exposed to a fungicide called carbendazim. As it happens, carbendazim is very similar to benomyl, the active ingredient in Benlate. DuPont's Benlate. Donna was contacted by John Ashton, a reporter for the *London Observer* who had been investigating the Scotland cases and he asked her if she'd been exposed to any agricultural chemicals. That's when she remembered that warm day walking past the strawberry and tomato farm. The owner of the farm was contacted and, sure enough, confirmed that the chemical Donna had been doused with that day was none other than Benlate.

Donna found herself an attorney, Jim Ferraro, who agreed to take on her case against DuPont, against all odds, just like Andy and Stan took on mine. And against all odds, Donna won. She and her husband were awarded $4 million, which, to me, seems almost like a loss. How much is sight worth? Nevertheless, DuPont did what DuPont does. Not content to live with a judgment that would have been pocket change to them and everything to Donna, they appealed. Eventually, the case went to the Florida Supreme Court where the verdict was upheld. DuPont paid the Castillos. The time from when the Castillos first took legal action until the Supreme Court ruling? More than ten years.[7]

Here's the thing about Benlate and birth defects: the connection was not unknown to DuPont. All the way back in 1972, the Environmental Protection Agency had advised DuPont to put a label on Benlate warning that it could cause birth defects and that "exposure during pregnancy should be avoided." But DuPont lobbied the EPA—successfully—that the warning was misleading and unnecessary, and so it never appeared.[8]

Moreover, one of DuPont's own reports indicated a health concern with Benlate. An independent laboratory in England tested benomyl on rats and found that a significant portion of the chemical was drawn to the eyes. In fact, after ten days, 80 percent of the benomyl ended up pooling around the eyes of the rats. Experimenting with rodents might not accurately reflect the risk to a full-grown human, but definitely might suggest a risk for a fetus. In the very early stages of pregnancy, the essential structures of a baby's eyes are just being formed. This is how scientists now believe Benlate can destroy the eyes of a fetus. The date on the report connecting eye issues with benomyl was 1997. The date of the Florida Supreme Court ruling? 2003. DuPont continued to fight the case six years after receiving a report that strongly suggested their chemical might well be responsible for Johnny Castillo's blindness.

Of course, we knew all about DuPont's insistent denials when it came to plant damage, but we didn't know that, as we were going to trial, DuPont was denying accusations about health issues, too. For growers like us, Benlate was a bad, bad chemical. Farmers complained about damage done by Benlate long after the alleged contamination took place. Lawsuits like ours dragged on everywhere, with DuPont kicking and screaming the whole way. The last figure I saw was that they had judgments against them from growers totaling $1.9 *billion*. The number of lawsuits was well over 800.

As far as lawsuits for crop damage are concerned, perhaps the most damaging from a PR standpoint was one from 2001. A Florida jury didn't just find DuPont liable for crop damage; they found them liable for racketeering, negligence, fraud, and defective product claims in a case filed by two Costa Rican plant nurseries.[9]

That case hinged on tests DuPont conducted itself in Costa Rica in 1992. The results of those tests? We can only guess. DuPont destroyed the records. According to the growers' attorney, "DuPont launched a corporate damage control program by assigning an attorney to supervise the testing, skewing some results and discarding those that were unfavorable." A plant pathologist from Penn State University was brought in and testified that DuPont's own documents—dating back to *1980!*—described Benlate as an unstable product prone to deterioration. Some plants treated with Benlate, the pathologist testified, grew to only 10 percent of their expected height, miniature roses in Florida dropped all of their leaves within two days of treatment, and (as we knew firsthand) Hawaiian orchids treated with Benlate were too malformed to sell.[10]

Stanley Tomono and I were lucky to have the attorneys we had, willing to risk everything and stick their necks out. We were also willing to hang in there ourselves, no matter the cost. Other farmers weren't as fortunate or didn't have the resources to continue. Steve Lindsey, a strawberry farmer in Plant City, Florida is just one example. Rather than drag himself through the entire process of a jury trial, he settled with DuPont. Unfortunately, they didn't pay enough for him to catch up on his debts. His farm was ruined and he had no means by which to recoup his losses. He sold his share of the farm even though it had been in his family since 1933. As he told the *St. Petersburg Times*, "They've got dozens of lawyers on retainer and billions to fight you. I'm a small man. How do I fight DuPont?"[11]

It's interesting to consider how a mega corporation like DuPont responds to so many lawsuits and complaints. If you ran a business and suddenly everybody was complaining about your product, you might be tempted to figure out what was going wrong and correct it. At the least, you might consider the possibility that the customers were right, that it was too coincidental for them all to be complaining about the same thing at once. But that's why you're not the CEO of DuPont. DuPont responded immediately by going on the defensive. They denied anything was wrong with Benlate. Hoping the problem would disappear, they quickly settled with some growers, but they grew to regret this strategy. In a 2006 interview with the *Associated Press*, Tom Sager, a DuPont vice president and assistant general counsel, lamented giving the growers the early benefit of the doubt. In his view, being too willing to settle (too willing, that is, to do the right thing and make recompense to the customer) only encouraged more lawsuits. "It wasn't an open checkbook," he said, "but there was not the kind of discipline and oversight we should have had in place." After that, DuPont developed a ten-step planning process for their litigation which included making sure their attorneys were all well-versed in product liability, and centralizing decision-making.[12] They circled the wagons, in other words. The primary concern became not the customer or the product, but how to better prepare for lawsuits. And, apparently, how to keep the denial going as long as possible.

But enough about Benlate and crop damage and birth defects. The good people of Parkersburg, West Virginia will tell you about another DuPont chemical: perfluorooctanoic acid, or PFOA. Until 2013, PFOA was used to make Teflon. But studies revealed a significant correlation between high PFOA exposure and kidney cancer, testicular cancer, ulcerative colitis, thyroid disease, and other health problems.[13] To DuPont, this was no new revelation. Leaked internal company documents showed that DuPont knew about some of the dangers of PFOA as far back as 1961. At that point, their own studies indicated that PFOA increased the size of the liver in rats, rabbits, and dogs.[14] In the 1970s, DuPont found that employees in its Parkersburg, West Virginia plant, where they made Teflon, had high concentrations of PFOA in their blood. In 1981, 3M, which supplied DuPont with the PFOA, informed DuPont that ingestion of PFOA causes birth defects in rats. DuPont subsequently tested recent newborns of their employees and found that of seven births, two had eye defects. In 1984, they discovered that dust emitted from their factory's chimneys drifted well beyond the factory and was found in the local water supply. In 1991, they discovered that in one district, PFOA levels three times DuPont's *own internal safety limit* were found in the drinking water.[15]

Naturally, this was all very unacceptable to DuPont and so like any good corporate citizen, they released all of this information to the EPA and to all the proper authorities, immediately ended their use of PFOA, and set about making sure the drinking water was cleaned up and the remaining PFOA was disposed of safely and properly. Or they would have done these things if they weren't more concerned with their bottom line. In truth, they did none of these things. In fact, they kept all of these findings to themselves and continued to manufacture Teflon with PFOA.

Now, it must be said that at very low levels, such as using your Teflon-coated frying pan to make an omelet, the long-term dangers of PFOA are debatable. The World Health Organization has classified it as "possibly carcinogenic to humans." The EPA has stated that there is "suggestive evidence of carcinogenicity." Enough is known, however, to make a reasonable person cringe at the thought of exposure at high levels. Yet high-level exposure is exactly what DuPont allowed to happen. In Parkersburg, between 1951 and 2003, DuPont dumped and emitted over *1.7 million pounds* of PFOA.[16]

In 1998, a family living near a DuPont landfill sued over the loss of their cattle. In all, 7,000 tons of PFOA sludge had been dumped on a sixty-acre plot of land adjacent to the farm. Cattle began acting deranged. Then they became sickly.

Then they started dying. The farmer, Earl Tennant, lost 153 head.[17] (The case was dramatized in the 2019 film *Dark Waters* starring Mark Ruffalo.) The suit was settled but it led to a rash of further suits. The attorney in the Tennant case, Robert Bilett, filed suit in 2001 on behalf of 80,000 people living where PFOA had leaked into the water supply. This was settled in 2005 with DuPont agreeing to provide up to $235 million for medical monitoring for over 70,000 people living in six water districts around the Parkersburg plant.

By 2014, there were many more individual lawsuits filed for PFOA-related diseases. Within a year, the number of cases rose to 3,500. Despite DuPont's denials, juries were finding them responsible for the cancers that plaintiffs were suing for. One jury found that DuPont had acted "with malice" and ordered them to pay $5.6 million in punitive and compensatory damages. By 2017, DuPont had finally had enough, settling over 3,550 cases for $671 million.

Nevertheless, they continue to deny any wrongdoing.

Cancers, birth defects, crop damage. For DuPont, the issue is one of risk versus reward. How much can you get away with before you eventually have to start paying someone? And will those payments be sufficient to negate the profits? Or is some expense simply just a part of doing business? At some point, either by order of the EPA or by the economics of the matter given the inevitable lawsuits, a particular product may have to be pulled from the shelves. It's a bottom-line financial decision, of course. A matter of profitability. The human cost? A nonfactor. For DuPont, it's all just business as usual.

TEN

The Lost Decade

For almost ten years, my life revolved around the DuPont trial. Of course, I wasn't alone. After the final settlement, Andy Wilson walked into his law office one morning and realized he had nothing to do. There were no cases. He and Stan Roehrig had focused all the firm's resources on my case and had to begin anew. Of course, they'd gotten quite a big chunk of the final award, so they were, once again, back on solid financial footing. They were able to pay off their debts and move forward. Finally, they could breathe again. For Stan's part, he had just turned fifty when I had originally come to him and Andy with my complaint against DuPont. He's still practicing at age eighty, and if you asked what he did during his fifties, he'll tell you he worked on a single case. Ten years of his life. But of course, that's the way it was for everyone involved. Ten years gone. Ten years spent on a legal action that never should have been necessary in the first place. Losing money is one thing. Can you put a price on someone's time, on whole years of someone's life?

It's worth asking who really won the case. DuPont committed fraud with the Alta documents and our jury never did get to consider the full import of the damage done to my soil by the sulfonylureas. I can only speculate, but my attorneys tell me that if the jury had awarded us monetary damages for the soil remediation, the award might have been a hundred million dollars or more. The fraud and withholding of evidence were just costs of business for DuPont, saving them those millions. It was a strategy, a cost/benefit calculation. Risk versus reward. And it paid off. It's interesting to consider that during the course of our legal action, the price of DuPont's stock rose by close to *70 percent.*

After the settlement, it was finally time for me to move on. But to where? My soil was contaminated. How long would it stay that way? Nobody knew. But I couldn't grow roses anymore. With my soil, I couldn't effectively grow anything. Nor could I sell the farm without disclosing the contamination. I suppose I could have answered any concerns a buyer might have by pointing toward the jury's decision and saying that they had not found sufficient cause for soil remediation damages, thus providing some kind of proof that my soil must be okay. But, at best, that would have been only a partial truth. And a partial lie. I knew the jury hadn't been given access to the information I had. In the end, selling the farm wasn't really an option.

Probably, I would have eventually been out of the rose business anyway. New competition was beginning to make things very difficult. By that time, most of the roses for sale on the wholesale market were coming from South America, chiefly Ecuador and Columbia, where labor was cheap. Transportation methods had improved, and South American growers could bring their product to market faster. They were now much more competitive than in years past. Roses were soon coming into the market from Africa, as well, with Ethiopia and Kenya becoming major exporters. The writing was on the wall.

I started thinking about a complete shift and began looking hard at tomatoes, a high-demand product, one of the most popular agricultural products in the world. But I also had to start thinking about a way to grow them given the inherent problems of my soil. Fortunately, I knew of a way, a way that wouldn't involve the soil at all: hydroponics. Hydroponics is a method of growing plants in water enriched with mineral nutrients. No soil required. The method had been around a while and had proven itself very successful, especially with tomatoes. I'd never considered hydroponics before, but now I had little choice.

The problem was, I knew next to nothing about the methodology and I had a lot of learning to do. The settlement had at least given me enough money to invest in the right equipment. The first thing we did was clean and sanitize the greenhouse, covering over all the soil with plastic. Then, to attain some practical education, it was back to the most knowledgeable place I knew of in the whole plant-growing world—the Netherlands. The Dutch didn't just know roses. Turns out, the "Land of Flowers" knew a thing or two about multiple crops. In fact, the country produces more tomatoes per square mile than anywhere else in the world.

In the process of buying hydroponic equipment from a supplier in Ontario, Canada, I was introduced to Peter Krul, a semiretired hydroponics expert living there but originally from the Netherlands. We took a trip to Amsterdam together and attended conferences and went on agricultural tours. Then Peter came back to Hawaii with me and spent six months helping me get the farm completely converted from a rose farm to a hydroponic tomato farm. It wasn't easy, but Peter was passionate about the work. It was his love. I gave him a place to stay and took care of his expenses, but in all the time he worked for me, he never asked for any money.

Peter and I had our differences, however. His passion for the work crossed the line into anger sometimes, and he could be exceptionally stubborn, too. At one point, I decided I couldn't work with him anymore and told him I thought it was time for him to go back to Ontario. He looked at me and said, "No. No, I'm not going back. I have a job to finish here first." And then he went back to whatever it was he was doing. What could I say?

Finally, we got everything up and going and the farm was in full production. Peter went back to Canada. Today, I have to give Peter Krul all the credit in the world for helping Kawamata Farms make the transition and I'm grateful he stuck around. Without his diligent efforts, I have no idea what might have happened with our farm. He's been back since and, with his help, we've expanded. More greenhouses. More tomatoes.

Fortunately, I did find a way to pay Peter back. A waitress I knew at a local restaurant asked me one day if I happened to know anyone who would make a good husband to her sister who was looking to come over from the Philippines. I said I did, and talked to Peter about her. Peter was lonely and looking for a female companion. Peter and my waitress friend's sister ended up connecting, one thing led to another, and, today, they're happily married and living in Ontario.

Although the tomato business is a good one, I must confess that I've never lost my love of roses. Growing something practical (and edible) is a great thing, but as far as I'm concerned, the beauty of a well-grown rose really can't be matched by a tomato. Others must feel the same way because on Valentine's Day, no one ever seems to want to give their love a dozen tomatoes. And from a farming standpoint, tomatoes are harder to grow, especially hydroponically. Soil is more forgiving than a hydroponic environment. (Assuming the soil's not contaminated, that is.) When you're growing in soil, you monitor the results and you react. With hydroponics, you have to be more proactive. You have to create the environment the product will grow in. You can forget to fertilize roses in the soil and they're still going to come out of the ground. Hydroponics is much more hands-on. You have to be constantly analyzing to make sure you're creating the right conditions for growth.

I won't complain, though. There was a time when the future of Kawamata Farms was in question. But after all these years, we're still going strong. There have been ups and downs, a lost decade, and a complete transformation of operations. But through it all, we're still here.

ELEVEN

What I Learned about the American Judicial System

In a Texas sexual harassment case against Walmart, the retail giant proceeded in such bad faith that the judge was moved to declare that, "Rarely has this Court seen such a pattern of deliberate obfuscation, delay, misrepresentation, and downright lying to another party and to a Court."[18]

In a suit in Illinois brought by a roofer against Shell Oil for asbestos-related cancer, a judge was sufficiently provoked by the defendant's conduct to pronounce it a "deliberate, contumacious, and unwarranted disregard of this Court's authority."[19]

In a case against General Motors for a fuel tank defect, a Georgia judge found GM guilty of obstructing justice and "committing fraud on the court."[20]

In a case against Ford for a defective seat that contributed, as a result of a traffic accident, to the brain damage of a two-year-old child, the car manufacturer behaved so deceitfully that the Michigan judge was moved to say that "'lied' would understate what Ford did," adding that, "an outrageous fraud has been perpetrated."[21]

What do these cases have in common? Two things. First, they represent prime examples of big corporations being caught trying to game the justice system. The sexual harassment case wasn't the first, or last, time Walmart had been caught. They've been sanctioned dozens of times for flouting the rules of discovery.[22] Shell Oil, in the case cited above, withheld over 100 boxes of relevant documents. General Motors, in the process of pretrial discovery, removed 2,300 documents without the court's permission. Ford concealed over 120,000 pages of relevant information.[23] Rightfully so, the judges in these cases acted correctly, admonishing and sanctioning the defendants just as Judge Ibarra sanctioned DuPont.

The second thing they have in common is more disheartening. These admonishments and sanctions seem to be the exception and not the rule. And it isn't because abusing the civil justice system is rare. Quite the opposite. Abusing the justice system is all too common, especially abusing the rules of discovery. What's rare is being caught and sanctioned for it. Large corporations like Walmart and Shell and GM and Ford (and DuPont, of course) have legal representation that understands the weaknesses of the system (the process of discovery, in particular) and how to exploit them. Most times, they get away with the exploitation. Not because they don't get caught, but because other than blatant obfuscation or downright lying, there really isn't anything preventing them from doing so. Judges have a surprising amount of discretion, but it seems to take an awful lot for a judge to interfere except for the most obvious and egregious cases of system abuse.

Carl Pacini has seen this reluctance in judges. A professor at the University of South Florida, and a lawyer, Dr. Pacini recently coauthored a paper on the abuses of discovery.[24] Along with professors William Hopwood and George Young of Florida Atlantic University, Dr. Pacini researched the pitfalls of discovery and a concluded that the process has become nothing less than "a tactical weapon." In the hands of unscrupulous attorneys, it has become "predatory."

Discovery, properly undertaken, is an important part of any civil procedure. The idea is for both sides to get a handle on the evidence that's going to be presented during the trial before the trial takes place. That way, there are no surprises in the courtroom. The idea of a "surprise witness," for instance, is really pretty rare. The theory is that each side be made aware of the other side's evidence, including witnesses, so that they can properly plan for it. But clever attorneys, like the ones in the above cases, use loopholes in the process to gain advantage.

In a recent interview with my editor, Dr. Pacini confessed that the reason for the unwillingness to sanction attorneys for abusing the system remains something of a mystery. "It may be a circle-the-wagons kind of thing, a judge not wanting to censure what is, in a sense, a fellow colleague, a fellow representative of the American judicial system. Or, perhaps, a judge might be hesitant because he or she might fear that the side being ruled against will file a motion saying that the judge abused his or her discretion, thus costing even more time and money."

As pointed out by Lawyers for Civil Justice and others in a whitepaper entitled "Reshaping the Rules of Civil Procedure for the 21st Century," it may also be that it is difficult at the beginning of a case for a judge "to determine the proper scope of discovery, because they know less than the parties about the underlying facts of each side's position."[25] Maybe so. But whatever the reason, the failure of judges to sanction attorneys and their clients for abusing the judicial system has made the situation ripe for even more and more abuse. The ultimate goal? To turn a court case into a war of attrition. It's not hard to guess who typically comes out on top in a war between a mega corporation and your everyday aggrieved citizen.

Dr. Pacini and his colleagues point out that discovery abuse typically takes one of two forms: excessive use to wear down an adversary, or stonewalling. In both cases, it means more time and effort is required, and time and effort equal money.

Excessive use can be employed in both directions. The requesting party can ask for everything under the sun, using, or rather overusing, tools the system makes available, like interrogatories (written questions the other party is required to answer), depositions, or requests to produce documents. If the requesting party wants to abuse these tools, it's relatively easy to do so. Basically, you just keep asking for stuff. If you need someone's bank records for a certain month, you ask for five years' worth. Conversely, the receiving party can use the strategy of excess in return, what Judge Ibarra called dump truck discovery. "You want a document? Fine. Here's 100,000 of them." According to one study, 4,980,441 pages of documents were produced in discovery during one recent year. The amount actually used in trial? 4,772.[26] It becomes a game. Unfortunately, it costs a lot of money to play.

Stonewalling can take various forms, from outright refusal to comply with a request to responding inadequately—providing only pieces of what's asked for or handing over something that's just not *quite* what the requesting party wanted. Then the requesting party has to ask again or file a motion with the court to make the court force the other party to comply. Often, judges grant continuances, giving the other party more time. Weeks and months and even years can go by while all of this is playing out. Sometimes, as in our case, a party can just flat out hold onto a piece of evidence in the hopes its existence never gets made public. Sanctions like Judge Ibarra's $1.5 million fine of DuPont are designed to discourage this. But if you're DuPont and you're being sued for multi-millions, not to mention the possibility of other suits and untold damage in the court of public opinion, what's $1.5 million? Not that we didn't appreciate the sanction and the message it sent, but DuPont's CEO probably has $1.5 million in pocket change.

There's a third type of discovery abuse, which is described by Pacini et al. as "obnoxious behavior by attorneys." Lawyers performing depositions have been known to harass witnesses with vulgar and abusive language and even physical threats. They might interrupt witnesses, constantly object, or become argumentative. The preferred strategy for these so-called "Rambo" litigators is to intimidate—both the witnesses as well as the opposing counsel.

Why is all of this allowed to take place? It might be because of the collective strength of corporate defense attorneys. The discovery process is part of the larger Federal Rules for Civil Procedure (FRCP), which govern the procedures of civil actions in United States district courts. The rules were initially established in 1938 and have been amended and tweaked several times over the years. Most recently, they were effectively rewritten in 2007 and substantially amended in 2009. The last time Title V of the FRCP—the portion that governs discovery—was amended was in 2015 and the amendment was made over the staunch objections of plaintiffs' attorneys throughout the land. Companies, mostly large corporations, had been complaining that in our new digital world, it was too much of a burden to make sure that electronic records (like emails, for instance) didn't accidentally get deleted. In the process of discovery, they'd be asked for records that they would claim had been electronic only (conveniently, no paper copies) and that had been unintentionally deleted from their computers. Whoops. "Sorry, we must have accidentally deleted that document."

After many sanctions had been levied against these companies (judges doing their jobs properly), corporate defense attorneys around the country got together and pushed through an amendment to Title V that limited sanctions on these "accidental" deletions (spoliation of evidence is the legal term) to the point where plaintiffs' attorneys say they can no longer effectively hold companies accountable for deleting key information.[27] Opposing counsel has to essentially prove that the other side *purposely* destroyed the electronic evidence to cover up their misdoings. But how does one prove an email or a compromising document was deleted on purpose? "You now have to catch the defendants red-handed to get any leverage," says plaintiff's attorney Brian Clark of Lockridge Grindal Nauen. "It's a nearly impossible standard to meet."[28] A longtime federal magistrate judge regarded as an expert on these matters, James Francis, has gone so far as to predict that the rule change "would curtail the ability of innocent parties to obtain relief."[29]

Can you imagine what would have happened if our case had been held today instead of in 1994? If DuPont's documents had been digital and not paper? Is it realistic to assume that if the missing documents for which Judge Ibarra sanctioned DuPont had been not hard copies but, say, PDFs within their computers that we would have ever seen them? Not only would DuPont not have been sanctioned, we might well have lost the case.

What can be done to fight these discovery abuses? There have been a few different proposals bandied about over the years. Dr. Pacini encourages the use of special masters, like the two retired judges in our case. According to Pacini, the special master should ideally be a forensic accountant, or even a team of forensic accountants, knowledgeable in the law, to sort through the ins and outs of the case and to "hold regularly scheduled hearings to address ongoing discovery disputes as they occur."[30] Federal judges have the discretion to do this. The problem is, if one of the parties to the case objects to the installment of such a special master, they can appeal the decision, arguing that the judge is abusing his discretion. After all, there's no rule under the FRCP that says a special discovery master is required. In many smaller cases, such a referee might not be needed. It's a judgment call, and judgment calls always carry with them the possibility of appeal. And that means more time gets wasted. And more money gets spent.

Another proposal is to allocate the costs of discovery to the one making the request. If one side is going to ask for every document that is even tangentially related to the case, that side has to pay for the costs thereof. According to the Lawyers for Civil Justice, a nonprofit advocacy group in Washington, DC, this "requester pays" rule would preserve the purpose of discovery—to permit parties to access information that will enable fact finders to determine the outcome of civil litigation—while aligning well-proven economic incentives with the reality of modern litigation.[31]

Although this would shift the cost, it still might not be enough to stop a company with deep pockets intent on engaging in predatory discovery. And no matter who pays, cases could still drag on. Regardless of who would have paid in our case, it still would have cost us years. What is time worth? Remember, unless the suit is purely frivolous, the goal of a war of attrition isn't to win in the court, it's to force the other side to capitulate to a settlement. Our outcome was the rare exception. Most plaintiffs end up willing to settle, probably for much less than they might receive if they have the resources to stick it out to the end. *Fewer than 3 percent* of civil cases reach a trial verdict.[32] Often, settlements are sealed, with the plaintiff precluded from revealing the amount of the settlement and with the defendant never admitting guilt or responsibility.

Neutral referees and "requester pays" rules are steps in the right direction, however. Can the FRCP be amended to require them? Well, the FRCP comes under the purview of the United States Supreme Court which can modify the procedures based on input from the Judicial Conference of the United States. The Conference was established in 1922 to provide guidelines for judicial courts and consists of the chief justice of the United States, the chief judge of each court of appeals federal regional circuit, a district court judge from various federal judicial districts, and the chief judge of the United States Court of International Trade. Proposed changes to the procedures from the Judicial Conference are subject to public comment and debate by interested parties. The problem is that almost nobody is more interested than the country's corporate defense attorneys, at least in a financial context. Corporate lawyers and trial attorneys are among the highest paid legal reps in the industry.[33] John Lacy was quoted as saying that he made more money than my attorneys on our case, even though he was the losing attorney! If you're defending a corporate behemoth like DuPont with a seemingly endless flow of funds, how likely are you to agree with a recommendation to amend the FRCP in a way that does damage to one of your main "tactical weapons"? It's revealing that the last major amendment—the 2015 amendment that limited sanctions on spoliation—was an amendment that helped, rather than hurt, corporate defenses. If you're wondering if Congress could step in and legislate an amendment to the FRCP, it's possible in theory, but this would doubtless result in a long Constitutional fight about separation of powers.

In fact, if anything, the current climate in legal reform favors the corporate defense side. "Tort reform" is a popular subject these days. Large corporations, especially insurers, as well as other corporate special interests, are proposing changes to the civil justice system that would reduce the ability of victims to sue and, if a lawsuit is successful, to cap the amount of damages. They claim that frivolous lawsuits are clogging the court system and juries are awarding outrageous sums of money to plaintiffs. We've all heard about the famous McDonald's case where a woman sued the fast food giant after they sold her the hot coffee she spilled on herself. And we're all familiar with the slimy "slip-and-fall" attorneys who convince people to sue corporations for unjustified millions. The truth, however, is that this simply doesn't represent reality. Tort cases (cases against a person or company that has caused harm, typically through negligence) account for only *4 percent* of the entire civil court caseload.[34] This is far from "clogging" the court system. And law firms have a built-in economic incentive not to take on frivolous lawsuits to begin with. My attorneys risked everything to keep my case going. Think they would have done that if they felt I was "frivolously" suing DuPont? About those "huge" jury awards: according to the National Center for State Courts, 75 percent of tort judgments are for less than $12,200.[35]

Oh, and by the way, here are a few facts about that McDonald's case. The plaintiff, 79-year-old Stella Liebeck spilled the coffee in her lap while trying to remove the lid. McDonald's sold its coffee at 180 to 190 degrees, even though the Shriner's Burn Institute in Cincinnati had published warnings to the franchise food industry that its members were unnecessarily causing serious scald burns by serving beverages above 130 degrees. When Ms. Liebeck was burned, McDonald's coffee had already burned more than 700 people, including infants. Liebeck received third-degree burns over 16 percent of her body, requiring skin grafting and a hospital stay of eight days. Here's the really interesting thing: Ms. Liebeck offered to settle with McDonald's for $20,000. They refused. Sound familiar? In the trial McDonald's essentially forced her into out of arrogance, the jury awarded her $2.7 million in punitive damages. The trial judge reduced the punitive damages to $480,000. And then began the appeal process. In the end, the parties ultimately settled for less, though we'll never know for how much since the settlement was confidential.[36]

Nevertheless, through industry-sponsored "think tanks," massive PR campaigns, and well-heeled lobbying firms, the corporate defense industry is making headway in limiting the rights of citizens to sue major corporations and collect the damages that they rightly should. For the time being, a plaintiff's best chance rests with a fair-minded judge who makes wise use of the discretion he or she is allowed. Where discovery is concerned, judges have been known to install discovery referees and judges have been known to force one side or the other to pay for the costs of discovery. The problem isn't that judges don't have this discretion; it's that most times they fail to use it. The Ronald Ibarras of the judicial world are the exception, not the rule, and until that changes, we're stuck with a system that rewards the guy with the deepest pockets, the guy who knows a tactical weapon when he sees it and knows how to use it. And given the momentum of tort reform, it might only get worse.

TWELVE

Was It Worth It?

Early in this book, I mentioned a question I'd recently been asked about my actions against DuPont: *Looking back, was it all worth it?* Given the eventually successful outcome, was the settlement worth the time and the money? Maybe, in the course of reading my narrative, you guessed my answer. You were right if you guessed that my answer was no.

No, it was not worth it.

Not by a longshot.

I made millions from the settlement. But I spent millions. More importantly, I spent ten years of my life, years that are gone forever. What could I have done with those ten years? What could I have done with the millions spent?

And this, of course, is the tragic consequence of our American judicial system, a system geared for, indeed, *designed* for those with deep pockets. Justice is skillfully manipulated by those in the best financial condition to do so. What I discovered was that justice is not blind, as you were no doubt taught in school. It is not impartial. It is not objective. It sees very clearly and willingly lends itself toward those who have the financial wherewithal to game it, and finesse it, and delay it.

In a word, the system is broken.

I don't pretend to know how to fix it. I'll leave that for better minds. But the system in its present state is clearly not functioning the way it was originally intended, and if my book has conveyed nothing else, my hope is that it has conveyed at least this. And keep this in mind: I am saying this as a person who *won* his case. Something is wrong when you win, yet still lose as much as I lost. And therein lies a tragic truth. If you're DuPont, if you have deep pockets, if you have seemingly unlimited resources, you can lose yet still win.

You can, in other words, simply be too big to lose.

Besides the legal system, a word must also be said about the morality of corporate America. DuPont is the bad guy in this book, but DuPont is far from alone, as we saw in the previous chapter. A nation needs to look itself in the mirror when its biggest corporate citizens routinely finagle that nation's justice system, even if that finagling is an inherent part of the system and, strictly speaking, legal. Are there not other values to answer to, higher values than what is merely "legal"? Does morality no longer play a part? Ethics? Did anyone, up and down the ladder of command at DuPont, ever once, during the entire Benlate scandal, ask, "What is the *right* thing for us to do?" The chairman, the corporate officers, the board of directors—did not even one person stand up and object to their organization's denials, delays, and deceptions? I can't help but wonder what is being taught in this country's business schools and MBA programs.

These days, I often find myself thinking back to our state motto and how true—literally true—that it is. *Ua mau ke ea o ka aina i ka pono.* "The life of the land is perpetuated in righteousness." I discovered firsthand that when we take away righteousness, we take away the life of the very soil from which we generate the means for our survival. Without a sense of honor and goodness, we're apparently left free to poison the land without fear of reprisal. It's true metaphorically as well, of course. We're all left a little contaminated, a little damaged. We're made worse as a people, and we're made worse because, societally, we can only ever be as good as our institutions. I want to believe that collectively we're better than our justice system, that we're better than DuPont. But if our justice system remains broken and if corporate greed continues to go unpunished and, indeed, even rewarded with higher stock values and executive bonuses, it's a damn hard belief to hang on to.

ACKNOWLEDGMENTS

First and foremost, my deep appreciation to my wife, Linda M. Kelly, for her relentless encouragement in getting this book written.

Additionally, there are many people who helped make this book possible, including those who fought the long battle with me. Special thanks to Stan Roehrig, Andy Wilson, Kris LaGuire, Steve Cox, and all the secretaries and assistants—my own "Dream Team."

Thanks to my partners in the case: Stanley Tomono and Cynthia Nakamoto. It helped to share the burden, financially and emotionally.

A special note of gratitude to the jury for their endless patience and for their ability and willingness to see through DuPont's duplicity. Your dedication and sacrifice through seven long months earned my undying respect. *Mahalo.*

I'd like to thank my ex-wife, Joanne, for her strength and patience during the trial.

My daughter, Leilyn, for always being there.

My gratitude to my editor, Jerry Payne, for helping me sort out all the material, much of it decades old, and for helping me get the words right.

Much appreciation to Carol Mast for her valuable input and friendship through the years.

Thanks as well to Joan Namkoong for her valued feedback.

Finally, a special thank you, in memory, to my very dear friend, Sandra (Schutte) Song.

NOTES

1 Hawaii Herald-Tribune, from *WSJ*, 4 May 1995.

2 *https://www.upi.com/Archives/1993/08/12/DuPont-settles-Benlate-DF-suit-out-of-court/8961745128000/*

3 *https://www.nytimes.com/1993/08/01/us/du-pont-s-enemy-in-lawsuit-its-own-papers.html*

4 *https://www.sun-sentinel.com/news/fl-xpm-1994-04-23-9404220808-story.html*

5 *https://www.courtlistener.com/opinion/71302/bush-ranch-v-e-i-dupont/*

6 Hawaii Tribune-Herald, 22 August 1995.

7 Ferraro, James. *Blindsided: The True Story of One Man's Crusade against Chemical Giant DuPont*, Gildan Media, 2017.

8 Barnett, Antony. "Eyeless Children Championed by Observer win $7M Test Case," *The Guardian*, 20 December 2003.

9 "DuPont Convicted of Racketeering in Benlate Case," Pesticide Action Network, *http://www.panna.org/legacy/panups/panup_20010817.dv.html.*

10 *Ibid.*

11 Levesque, William. "Benlate's Bitter Legacy," *St. Petersburg Times*, 24 September 2006.

12 Chase, Randall. "DuPont Grapples with Legacy of Benlate," *Houston Chronicle*, 20 March 2006.

13 Nicole, Wendee. "PFOA and Cancer in a Highly Exposed Community: New Findings from the C8 Science Panel," *Environmental Health Perspectives*, Nov–Dec., 2013.

14 Kourabas, Michael. "The Case of DuPont's Pollution," Web, 11 Jan 2016.

15 *Ibid.*

16 Board, Glynis. "Ohio River Communities are Still Coping with Teflon's Toxic Legacy," Web, 20 July 2017.

17 Kourabas, Michael

18 Van Voris, Bob. "Wal-Mart Cited for Discovery Abuse," *National Law Journal*, 3 May 1999, p. A01.

19 *Hutcheson v. Shell Wood River Refining Co. et al.*, No. 99-L 450 (Madison County Cir. Ct., Ill., verdict May 20, 2000).

20 *Bampoe-Parry v. General Motors Corp.*, No. 98VS138297 (Fulton County Ct., Ga., order September 7, 1999).

21 *Traxler v. Ford Motor Co.*, 227 Mich. App. 276 (1998).

22 "How Corporations Abuse Our Civil Justice System," Center for Justice and Democracy.

23 These cases are nicely summarized in "How Corporations Abuse Our Civil Justice System," by the Center for Justice and Democracy, *http://centerjd.org*.

24 "Fighting Discovery Abuse in Litigation," C. Pacini, W. Hopwood, and G. Young. *Journal of Forensic & Investigative Accounting* v. 6, Issue 2, July–December 2014.

25 "Reshaping the Rules of Civil Procedure for the 21st Century: The Need for Clear, Concise, and Meaningful Amendments to Key Rules of Civil Procedure," submitted to the 2010 Conference on Civil Litigation, Duke Law School May 10–11, 2010, on behalf of Lawyers for Civil Justice, DRI—The Voice of the Defense Bar, Federation of Defense & Corporate Counsel, International Association of Defense Counsel.

26 "Litigation Cost Survey of Major Companies," statement submitted by Lawyers for Civil Justice, Civil Justice Reform Group, & US

Chamber Institute for Legal Reform for Presentation to *Committee on Rules of Practice and Procedure Judicial Conference of the United States* 2010 Conference on Civil Litigation.

27 "How Corporate Lawyers Made It Harder to Punish Companies That Destroy Electronic Evidence," ProPublica, Web, Will Young, 27 January 2020.

28 *Ibid.*

29 *Ibid.*

30 "Fighting Discovery Abuse in Litigation," C. Pacini, W. Hopwood, and G. Young. *Journal of Forensic & Investigative Accounting* v. 6, Issue 2, July–December 2014.

31 *https://www.lfcj.com/allocate-discovery-costs.html*

32 "A Profile of Settlement," *Court Review* v. 42, Issue 3–4, J. Barkai, E. Kent, P. Martin, Dec. 2006

33 *https://moneyinc.com/the-five-types-of-lawyers-that-make-the-most-money/*

34 National Center for State Courts, *State Court Caseload Digest: 2017 Data* (2019)

35 "The Landscape of Civil Litigation in State Courts," National Center for State Courts November 2015.

36 The Center for Justice & Democracy at New York Law School. http://centerjd.org/